First World War
and Army of Occupation
War Diary
France, Belgium and Germany

30 DIVISION
90 Infantry Brigade
Royal Scots Fusiliers
2nd Battalion
1 January 1916 - 31 March 1918

WO95/2340/1

The Naval & Military Press Ltd
www.nmarchive.com
Published in association with The National Archives

Published by

The Naval & Military Press Ltd

Unit 10 Ridgewood Industrial Park,

Uckfield, East Sussex,

TN22 5QE England

Tel: +44 (0) 1825 749494

www.naval-military-press.com

www.nmarchive.com

This diary has been reprinted in facsimile from the original. Any imperfections are inevitably reproduced and the quality may fall short of modern type and cartographic standards.

© **Crown Copyright**
Images reproduced by permission of The National Archives, London, England, 2015.

Contents

Document type	Place/Title	Date From	Date To
Heading	WO95/2340 2/R Scots Fus. Jan '16-Mar '18		
Heading	30th Division 90th Infy Bde 2nd Bn Roy. Scots Fus. Jan 1916-Mar 1918 From 7 Div 21 Bde To 9 Div S African Bde		
Heading	2 R Scots Fuel 901/20 Jan Vol XIV 9th Bde Jan 16-Mar 18		
War Diary		01/01/1916	07/01/1916
War Diary	Suzanne Trenches	08/01/1916	08/01/1916
War Diary	Trenches	09/01/1916	12/01/1916
War Diary	Suzanne	13/01/1916	16/01/1916
War Diary	Trenches	16/01/1916	20/01/1916
War Diary	Maricourt	21/01/1916	24/01/1916
War Diary	Trenches	25/01/1916	29/01/1916
War Diary	A2 Sector	29/01/1916	01/02/1916
War Diary	Suzanne	02/02/1916	07/02/1916
War Diary	Trenches A2	07/02/1916	15/02/1916
War Diary	Trenches	16/02/1916	19/02/1916
War Diary	Suzanne	20/02/1916	27/02/1916
War Diary	Trenches	28/02/1916	29/02/1916
Heading	2 R Scots Fus Vol XVI		
War Diary		01/03/1916	11/03/1916
War Diary	Y2 Sector	12/03/1916	19/03/1916
War Diary	Camp Etinehem	20/03/1916	28/03/1916
War Diary	Flixecourt	29/03/1916	31/03/1916
Heading	2 R Scots Fus Vol XVII		
War Diary	Flixecourt	01/04/1916	24/04/1916
War Diary	Coissy	25/04/1916	30/04/1916
War Diary	Trenches	01/05/1916	31/05/1916
War Diary	Bray	01/06/1916	11/06/1916
War Diary	Trenches	12/06/1916	15/06/1916
War Diary	In Trenches	16/06/1916	18/06/1916
War Diary	Briquesmesnil	19/06/1916	26/06/1916
War Diary	Etinehem	27/06/1916	30/06/1916
Heading	War Diary of 2nd. Bn. Royal Scots. Fusiliers. for July 1916		
War Diary	Assembly Trenches	01/07/1916	01/07/1916
War Diary	Montauban	01/07/1916	03/07/1916
War Diary	Happy Valley	04/07/1916	09/07/1916
War Diary	Malt Horn Trench	09/07/1916	10/07/1916
War Diary	Malt Horn Farm	10/07/1916	11/07/1916
War Diary	Bois Celestins	12/07/1916	13/07/1916
War Diary	Daours	14/07/1916	20/07/1916
War Diary	Happy Valley	21/07/1916	27/07/1916
War Diary	Carnoy	28/07/1916	31/07/1916
Heading	90th Brigade. 30th Division. 2nd Battalion Royal Scots Fusiliers August 1916		
War Diary	Happy Valley	01/08/1916	02/08/1916
War Diary	Longpre	03/08/1916	04/08/1916
War Diary	Berguette	05/08/1916	05/08/1916
War Diary	L'Ecleme	06/08/1916	11/08/1916

War Diary	Bethune	12/08/1916	31/08/1916
Heading	War Diary. For the month of September 1916. 2nd Battalion Royal Scots Fusiliers. Volume 3 Vol 22		
War Diary	Bethune	01/09/1916	03/09/1916
War Diary	Trenches	04/09/1916	14/09/1916
War Diary	Le Touret	15/09/1916	16/09/1916
War Diary	Essars	17/09/1916	17/09/1916
War Diary	M. Bernenchon	18/09/1916	18/09/1916
War Diary	Beauval	18/09/1916	21/09/1916
War Diary	Flesselles	22/09/1916	30/09/1916
Heading	War Diary. For the month of October 1916. 2nd Bn Royal Scots Fusiliers. Volume 3 Vol 23		
War Diary	Flesselles	01/10/1916	10/10/1916
War Diary	Trenches	10/10/1916	22/10/1916
War Diary	Ribemont	23/10/1916	26/10/1916
War Diary	Doullens	27/10/1916	27/10/1916
War Diary	Warluzel	28/10/1916	29/10/1916
War Diary	Bailleulval	30/10/1916	30/10/1916
War Diary	Trenches	31/10/1916	31/10/1916
Heading	War Diary For The Month Of November 1916. 2nd Battalion Royal Scots Fusiliers. Volume 3 Vol 24		
War Diary	Trenches	01/11/1916	06/11/1916
War Diary	Bellacourt	07/11/1916	12/11/1916
War Diary	Trenches	13/11/1916	18/11/1916
War Diary	Bailleulval & Basseux	19/11/1916	24/11/1916
War Diary	Trenches	25/11/1916	30/11/1916
Heading	War Diary For The Month Of December 1916. 2nd Bn Royal Scots Fusiliers. Volume 3 Vol 25		
War Diary	Bellacourt	01/12/1916	06/12/1916
War Diary	Trenches	07/12/1916	12/12/1916
War Diary	Bailleulval & Basseux	13/12/1916	17/12/1916
War Diary	Trenches	18/12/1916	24/12/1916
War Diary	Bellacourt	25/12/1916	29/12/1916
War Diary	Trenches	30/12/1916	31/12/1916
Heading	War Diary. For The Month Of January, 1917. 2nd Bn. Royal Scots Fusiliers. Volume 3 Vol 26		
War Diary	Trenches	01/01/1917	03/01/1917
War Diary	Bellacourt	04/01/1917	06/01/1917
War Diary	Bellacourt to Humbercourt	07/01/1917	07/01/1917
War Diary	Humbercourt	08/01/1917	30/01/1917
War Diary	Autieule	31/01/1917	31/01/1917
Heading	War Diary For The Month Of February, 1917 2nd Bn. Royal Scots Fusiliers. Volume 3 Vol 27		
War Diary	Authieule	01/02/1917	03/02/1917
War Diary	Mondicourt	04/02/1917	28/02/1917
Heading	War Diary For The Month Of March, 1917. 2nd Bn. Royal Scots Fusiliers. Volume 3 Vol 28		
War Diary	Mondicourt	01/03/1917	17/03/1917
War Diary	In the Field	18/03/1917	31/03/1917
Heading	War Diary, For The Month Of April 1917. 2nd Bn. Royal Scots Fusiliers. Volume 3 Vol 29		
War Diary	In the Field	01/04/1917	30/04/1917
Heading	War Diary For The Month Of May, 1917. 2nd Bn. Royal Scots Fusiliers. Volume 3 Vol 30		
War Diary	In the Field	01/05/1917	17/05/1917
War Diary	Vacqueriette	18/05/1917	20/05/1917

War Diary	Hericourt	21/05/1917	21/05/1917
War Diary	Tangry	22/05/1917	22/05/1917
War Diary	Rely	23/05/1917	24/05/1917
War Diary	Lambres	25/05/1917	25/05/1917
War Diary	La Kreule	26/05/1917	31/05/1917
Heading	War Diary For The Month Of June, 1917. 2nd Bn. Royal Scots Fusiliers. Volume 3 Vol 31		
War Diary	Moringhem	01/06/1917	06/06/1917
War Diary	Arbre	07/06/1917	08/06/1917
War Diary	In the Field	09/06/1917	30/06/1917
Heading	War Diary For The Month Of July 1917. 2nd Bn. Royal Scots Fusiliers. Volume 3 Vol 32		
War Diary	In the Field	01/07/1917	31/07/1917
Heading	War Diary of the 2nd Battalion, Royal Scots Fusiliers for the month of August 1917 Volume (3) Vol 33		
War Diary	In the Field	01/08/1917	31/08/1917
Heading	War Diary. for September 1917. 2nd Bn. Royal Scots Fusiliers. Vol 34		
War Diary	In the Field	01/09/1917	22/09/1917
War Diary	In Field	23/09/1917	28/09/1917
War Diary	Field	28/09/1917	30/09/1917
War Diary		01/09/1917	02/09/1917
War Diary	In Field	23/09/1917	24/09/1917
Heading	War Diary For October 1917. 2nd Bn. Royal Scots Fusiliers. Vol 35		
War Diary	In the Field	05/10/1917	31/10/1917
Heading	War Diary. for November 1917 2nd Bn. Royal Scots Fusiliers. Vol 36		
Heading	War Diary. for November 1917 2nd Bn. Royal Scots Fusiliers. Volume X		
War Diary		01/11/1917	04/11/1917
War Diary		01/11/1917	30/11/1917
Heading	War Diary Of The 2nd Battalion Royal Scots Fusiliers. For The Month Of December 1917. Volume 3 Vol 37		
War Diary	In the Field	01/12/1917	31/12/1917
Heading	War Diary Of The 2nd. Bn. Royal Scots Fusiliers. For Period. January 1-31st 1918 Volume 3 Vol 38		
War Diary	In the Field	01/01/1918	31/01/1918
Heading	War Diary of the 2nd Battalion Royal Scots Fusiliers. For The Month Of February 1918 Volume 3 Vol 39		
War Diary	In the Field	01/02/1918	23/02/1918
Heading	90th Inf. Bde. 30th Div. 2nd Battn. The Royal Scots Fusiliers. March 1918		
Heading	2 R Scot Fus Feb Vol XV		
Heading	War Diary Of The 2nd Battalion Royal Scots Fusiliers. For The Month Of March 1918 Volume 3 Vol 40		
War Diary	In the Field	01/03/1918	31/03/1918
Heading	WO95/2340 2/14 London (London Scottish) Jun '18-Aug '19		

WO 95/2340
2/R. Scots Fus.
Jan '16 – Mar '18

30TH DIVISION
90TH INFY BDE

WO95-2340

2ND BN ROY. SCOTS FUS.
JAN 1916 - MAR 1918

FROM 7 DIV 21 BDE
TO 9 DIV S AFRICAN BDE

2340

J R Scot- Ancl 90½/30

Jan / Vol XIV

15.A.

q B de

Jan 16
/
Mar 18

/ Army Form C. 2118.

WAR DIARY
or
INTELLIGENCE SUMMARY.
(Erase heading not required.)

Instructions regarding War Diaries and Intelligence Summaries are contained in F. S. Regs., Part II. and the Staff Manual respectively. Title pages will be prepared in manuscript.

Place	Date	Hour	Summary of Events and Information	Remarks and references to Appendices
	JANUARY 1916			AMIENS sheet 12. 1/80,000
	1-1-16		In Billets. C.O. inspected the Balln.	
	2-1-16		In Billets	
	3-1-16		In Billets	
	4-1-16		Bn marched to billets at TALMAS at 10.30 am via HAVERNAS - NAOURS.	
	5-1-16		Bn marches to billets at LA HOUSSOYE via SEPTENVILLE - PUCHEVILLERS - MOLLIENS au BOIS - ST GRATIEN. Arriving at 3pm. Distance 12 miles. The Bn marches in No 3 Column (Lt Col B C Fairfax) O.C. 17th K.L. Regt), but left the Column at MOLLIENS au BOIS.	
	6-1-16		Bn marches to billets at CHIPILLY & STINEHAM. Distance 12 miles, arriving at 3pm via Luce (River) Road. - A+B Co billeted at CHIPILLY. Remainder of Bn at STINEHAM. 1 Officer +1 NCO per Coy proceeds to trenches to take over stores etc. 1 Officer in addition to O.R.M.K. & his staff proceed to SUZANNE to billet the Batt.	ALBERT Contoui sheet 1/40,000
	7-1-16		Bn marches to SUZANNE at 4.30 pm via BRAY - CAPPY, arriving at 6.30pm. The Batt. relieves 1st A.O.C. 4th Int Bn till 12 noon 11th inst. Welsh returned from leave. Bn under orders 9 G.O.C. 4th Int Bde	

WAR DIARY or INTELLIGENCE SUMMARY

Army Form C. 2118.

Place	Date	Hour	Summary of Events and Information	Remarks and references to Appendices
SUZANNE	8-1-16		In Billets at SUZANNE. Draft of 34 other Ranks joined the Bn from 3/R.S.F. Bn moves to Trenches to relieve 12th Gloucesters in A2 Sector. Relief Completed by 10pm. Bn disposed as follows. A Coy Right Front. B Coy Left Front. C Coy Support with 2 Platoons in RAVINE and 2 Platoons in "S" Shelters. D Coy in Reserve at Bn H.Qrs. All M.Guns in Front Line as well as 4 Guns under Bde orders. 15th R. Warwickshire Regt. on our Left. 9th Royal Scots on our Right. Night Quiet. Nothing of importance occurred.	ALBERT (Combined Sheet) 1/40,000. Trench Map 62c NW1. 1/40,000
TRENCHES		A2		
Trenches	9-1-16		In Trenches. Quiet nothing to report. 16th Manchesters on Left & 18th Manchesters on Right.	
-do-	10-1-16		In Trenches. Hostile Snipers active to which we replied.	
-do-	11-1-16		In Trenches. Considerable Artillery activity in the afternoon. Wet day. The enemy's attention being directed against MARICOURT DEFENCES. Our Guns active also. Our Front trenches were somewhat heavily shelled during the afternoon. No Casualties. One 5.9 shell burst right into a dug out but failed to explode. 15 men were in the dug out at the time.	
	12-1-16		The day was much quieter on the whole. The enemy shelled SUZANNE afterwards being the day but apparently did no damage. The 2nd BEDFORDS relieves the Bn in the Evening at 5.30pm. Relief Completed by 8.30pm. Coys marched independently to billets in SUZANNE	

WAR DIARY or INTELLIGENCE SUMMARY

Army Form C. 2118.

Place	Date	Hour	Summary of Events and Information	Remarks and references to Appendices
SUZANNE	13-1-16		In Redt Reserve in Billets at SUZANNE. About 4 Shrapnel Shells burst near Headquarters. 1 Man slightly wounded.	ALBERT Confrnt Sheet 57d NW
	14-1-16 do-		In Billets SUZANNE. Enemy Shelled the town heavily from 11 am – 4 pm with intervals. Shells chiefly 5.9 Calibre, burst round the Church. Considerable damage was done. D Coy Sappers Bay heavily, having 6 men killed, 1 Died of wounds, 19 other ranks wounded. 1 Cavalier in C Coy. the C.S.M. being wounded. Total 27 (killed + wounded) Men. D Coy men very unlucky, ten shell bursting in a platoon's billet forcing through the Cellar where the majority of the Casualties of Coy. Commenced at once to dig trenches to shelter men from shells.	
	15-1-16 do		In Billets. No hostile Shelling. Coys men working all day in the trenches begun the previous day.	
16-1-16 Fo Trench-			In Billets. No shelling. At 3:30 pm the Bn moved by Coys to relieve the 2/Bedford Regt in A+B Sects. A Battery near SUZANNE was being heavily shelled + which always the 7 advance parties of the Bn a little. Relief Completed by 8.15 pm. Bn was disposed as follows. D Right Front. C Coy Left Front. ½ B Coy in RAVINE	

Army Form C. 2118.

WAR DIARY
or
INTELLIGENCE SUMMARY.
(Erase heading not required.)

Place	Date	Hour	Summary of Events and Information	Remarks and references to Appendices
Trenches	16-1-16		Army Reserve. Remainder of B Coy men attached, one platoon to each Front Coy. The London Gazette dated 14th inst publishes a list of decorations awarded. The undermentioned Officers & NCOs have awarded the decorations stated against their names for distinguished service in the Field, to date from 1/1/16. Captain. D.S.C. Critchley-Salmonson Military Cross. Captain G.R.T. Kennedy " " Lieut C. Wham Brown " " No 8387 C.Sgt Major J. Barnes Distinguished Conduct Medal. No 6963 Sgt J. Reilly - " " No 7661 Sgt J. McMullan " " No 14295 Cpl F. McCandlish " "	
	17-1-16		In Trenches. Night Quiet. An Enemy Aeroplane Crossed our Lines about 9am. Otherwise all quiet.	

Army Form C. 2118.

WAR DIARY
or
INTELLIGENCE SUMMARY.
(Erase heading not required.)

Instructions regarding War Diaries and Intelligence Summaries are contained in F. S. Regs., Part II. and the Staff Manual respectively. Title pages will be prepared in manuscript.

Place	Date	Hour	Summary of Events and Information	Remarks and references to Appendices
Trenches	18-1-16		In trenches. Day & night quiet. Some shelling at 6th Divis. Parapet of Scheme and #13 trench was damaged but repaired during the night. 1 Man wounded.	ALBERT contd Sheet 1/40000 Trench Map MARICOURT 1/10,000
	19-1-16		In trenches. Parapet of 13 trench again knocked in by a light shrapnel shell (42). Several Rifle Grenades were put over from Y wood during the night and early morning. About 20 light shrapnel were fired into left section of R&F front in the morning. No damage done. Enemy could be heard working on	
	do		their Cap in front of 17 trench during the night. 18th Manchesters on our Right, and 16th Manchesters on our Left.	
	20-1-16		Quiet night & day. 2 Bedfords relieved the Batt'n in A.2 Sect'n. Relief complete by 6.50pm. Batt'n moved into MARICOURT DEFENCES, Relieves 17 MANCHESTERS 16 MANCHESTERS Coys billets in houses. Each Coy with special bounds to hold in case of attack.	
MARICOURT	21-1-16		In MARICOURT. Quiet day. About 4pm Enemy shelled MARICOURT - SUZANNE Road with heavy Shrapnel. About 40-50 shells in all. Night quiet. Bn in MARICOURT DEFENCES is required to furnish 3 fatigues of 80 men each to work under 184th Tunnelling Coy R.E. Times 7.45am, 3.45pm & 11.45pm.	

WAR DIARY
or
INTELLIGENCE SUMMARY.

(Erase heading not required.)

Army Form C. 2118.

Place	Date	Hour	Summary of Events and Information	Remarks and references to Appendices
	22-1-16		In MARICOURT. Quiet morning. Enemy guns active in direction of SUZANNE.	ALBERT Cambrai Sheet 1/40,000. Trench Map MARICOURT 1/10,000.
MARICOURT.	23-1-16		In MARICOURT. Slight artillery activity. One enemy aeroplane active in morning.	
do.	24-1-16		17TH K LIVERPOOL REGT. relieved 2. R.S.F. in MARICOURT DEFENCES. 2.R.S.F. relieved 2ND BEDFORDS in A2 Subsector relief completed by 9.30 P.M. Very quiet day.	
do.	25-1-16		In trenches. Night quiet. Enemy observation balloon 26° mag over MARICOURT + another 141° mag. Slight artillery activity.	
Trenches.	26-1-16		In trenches. Enemy observation balloon over MARICOURT for a short time. Enemy shelled road SUZANNE - MARICOURT + CALVAIRE at night. Coy relief. C+D relieving A+B Coy.	
do.	27-1-16		In trenches. Slight artillery activity during day & early night.	
	28-1-16		Unusual artillery activity of enemy during night. At 6.15 A.M. heavy bombardment of MARICOURT + vicinity with both light & lachrymatory shells. Communication trenches + Bn H.Q. occupied vicinity shelled throughout day with Shrapnel & lachrymatory shells. SUZANNE + SUZANNE - MARICOURT roads + valley heavily bombarded with shrapnel 5.9 H.E. + Small gas shells. Relief of Bn in A sector cancelled. Small attack on FARGNY MILL defeated by 18TH MANCHESTERS. One prisoner of 63rd Regt. captured. Considerable shelling throughout night. 2/R.S.F. 2 slightly wounded.	
	29-1-16		Quiet in MARICOURT district throughout the day except for few small "tear" shells. Front + support line + communication trenches heavily shelled at intervals. Heavy cannonade on our right. SUZANNE + CAPPY + roads heavily shelled. Railway again [illegible].	

2353 Wt. W2514/1454 700,000 5/15 D. D. & L. A.D.S.S./Forms/C. 2118.

Army Form C. 2118.

WAR DIARY
or
INTELLIGENCE SUMMARY.
(Erase heading not required.)

Instructions regarding War Diaries and Intelligence Summaries are contained in F. S. Regs. Part II. and the Staff Manual respectively. Title pages will be prepared in manuscript.

Place	Date	Hour	Summary of Events and Information	Remarks and references to Appendices
A2 SECTOR	29-1-16		Bde report ran as follows: German G.O.C. FRISE last night. We hold roughly line E. of CANAL DE LA SOMME, BOIS DE LA VACHE + G.29.d.8.1. Co have reinforced French left S. of CANAL + strong reinforcements of artillery are arriving. 90th Inf. Bde.	ALBERT Combined Sheet 340,000 French Mat. MARICOURT 1/10,000
	30-1-16 do.		Zeppelin raided over MARICOURT at 1.A.M. + again at 2.A.M. Some heavy shells fell into SOZANNE in the morning. A few lachrymatory shells fell into MARICOURT + vicinity otherwise quiet on our front. Heavy cannonade towards FRISE. GAS alarm at 3.P.M. which proved to be false. Very quiet during night.	
	31.1.16		MARICOURT intensely shelled with "coal boxes" shells for ten minutes at 11.53.A.M. Very quiet in our SECTOR. Heavy cannonade at FRISE. Bde. report saw as follows:- The French regained part of the communication trench acq. Rest of line same as yesterday aas. Germans dug up in front of captured trenches aaa."	

N. Watson
LIEUT. COLONEL,
COMDG. 2nd ROYAL SCOTS FUSILIERS.

WAR DIARY
or
INTELLIGENCE SUMMARY.
(Erase heading not required.)

Army Form C. 2118.

Place	Date	Hour	Summary of Events and Information	Remarks and references to Appendices
A2 SECTOR	1-2-16		Very quiet night & day. Intermittent heavy cannonading towards FRISE. D Coy 2/R.S.F on left front relieved by C Coy of 2nd BEDFORD R.	ALBERT. Combined sheet 1/40,000. Trench Map 1/10,000 MARICOURT
SUZANNE	2-2-16 do.		Very quiet on our front with occasional heavy firing in direction of FRISE. Bn — with exception of two platoons of C Coy left in R WORKS — was relieved by 2nd BEDFORD R. at 5.30 P.M. Relief complete by 8 P.M. Bn moved to billets & dug-outs at SUZANNE.	
SUZANNE	3-2-16		In Billets. Dug outs. Coys. Inspected at improving their dug outs & shelters.	
	4-2-16 do.		In Billets. Dug outs. Considerable Artillery activity on both sides. Hostile guns shelled SUZANNE /mn about 12.30 pm — 2 pm. 2 men slightly wounded. No great damage done. Working party 1/50 men assisting Pioneer Coy (South Lancs Regt) in making dug outs & villages near NORTH ST. 1 officer & 40 men detailed for work under R.E.	
	5-2-16 do.		In Billets & Dug outs. Quiet day. No hostile shelling of SUZANNE	
	6-2-16 do.		In Billets. Dug outs. Considerable artillery activity South of R. SOMME. Enemy shelled outskirts of our SUZANNE about 2.30 pm.	
	7-2-16 do.		Enemy fired a few gas shells into SUZANNE about 2 pm. Bn relieved 2/Bedfords in A2 Sector at 5 pm. Relief Complete by 8.15 pm. Bn disposed as follows. D Coy Right Front. C Coy Left Front.	

Army Form C. 2118.

WAR DIARY
or
INTELLIGENCE SUMMARY.
(Erase heading not required.)

Instructions regarding War Diaries and Intelligence Summaries are contained in F.S. Regs., Part II. and the Staff Manual respectively. Title pages will be prepared in manuscript.

Place	Date	Hour	Summary of Events and Information	Remarks and references to Appendices
Trenches A2	7-2-16		B Coy had 2 Platoons in Support & remainder with 2nd Front Coy. A Coy Reserve with 2 platoons in RAVINE (R. Hooks) + 2 platoons at Bn. H.Q. 2 Platoons 17th K. Liverpool Regt. attached as Reserve at Bn.H.Q. Quiet night. Heavy fires for Ops Staff. 2nd Lt W.M. Syfret admitted to Field Ambulance.	ALBERT contains shut YPRES. Trench Map MARICOURT 1/10,000.
	8-2-16 do-		In trenches. Enemy Artillery Activity. Trenches were shelled but not much damage was done. 3 hostile Observation Balloons up. Night Quiet.	
	9-2-16 do-		In trenches. Quiet morning early. Enemy Artillery active on left in PERONNE ROAD and in Ayit towards SUZANNE. 4 hostile Observation Balloons up. Working party 4.1 platoon each digging a new trench between 15 + 16 Streets and making dug outs at junction of RAVINE with trench leading to 14, 15, 16 trenches. 18th MANCHESTERS on our Right. 16th MANCHESTERS on left.	
	10-2-16 do-		About midnight 9/10 inst, the enemy shelled SUZANNE and the vicinity very heavily, about 100 shells 7.5-9 calibre. The day was quiet.	
	11-2-16 do		2nd Lt W.L. Hay, 13th Scottish Rifles, joined the Battn for duty from England. The Bn was relieved by 2 Bedford in A2 Sector Commencing 5 pm. Relief Complete by 9.15pm. After Relief his Bn was disposed as follows. Hd Qrs in SUZANNE	

Army Form C. 2118.

WAR DIARY
or
INTELLIGENCE SUMMARY.
(Erase heading not required.)

Instructions regarding War Diaries and Intelligence Summaries are contained in F. S. Regs., Part II. and the Staff Manual respectively. Title pages will be prepared in manuscript.

Place	Date	Hour	Summary of Events and Information	Remarks and references to Appendices
	11-2-16		A Coy in ROYAL DRAGOONS } under command of Capt Bury. 18th MANCHESTERS.	West Central Sheet 57dSW Trench Map (MARICOURT) 1/10000.
	do		B Coy in " "	
			C Coy in U Works (MARICOURT DEFENCES)	
			D Coy { 2 platoons in R. Works (RAVINE) under OC A 2 Sector.	
			{ 2 platoons in BATTLE DUGOUTS under OC ROYAL DRAGOONS.	
	12-2-16		Battn disposed as above. Quiet day.	
	13-2-16		Battn disposed as above. Considerable Artillery activity South of R. SOMME. The French	
	do -		attacked & regained their lost trenches. Hostile guns of 5.9 calibre shelled SUZANNE for about 3¼ hours with intervals. About 200 shells in all, coming from an Easterly direction. The Signallers & Police cellar was hit. The occupants received slightly bruises. One policeman badly bruised in the shoulder. Considerable damage was done to houses and there were about 20 casualties in SUZANNE as result of the bombardment.	
	14-2-16		Battn disposed as above. Quiet day. Artillery on both sides less active.	
	do -			
	15-2-16		Bn disposed as above. Quiet day.	
	do -			

Army Form C. 2118.

WAR DIARY
or
INTELLIGENCE SUMMARY.
(Erase heading not required.)

Instructions regarding War Diaries and Intelligence Summaries are contained in F. S. Regs., Part II. and the Staff Manual respectively. Title pages will be prepared in manuscript.

Place	Date	Hour	Summary of Events and Information	Remarks and references to Appendices
Trenches	16-2-16		Quiet day. Extract from London Gazette dated 14/2/16 R.S.F. Temp 2/Lt D.H. Kennedy to be Temp Lieut Supernumerary to Staff: dated Nov 29th 1915. Bn relieve 2/Bedfords in A.2. Sector. Relief Complete by 1 a.m. 17th. Bn disposed as follows. A Coy Left Front. B Coy Right Front. C Coy 2 platoons in Support to Front Coys. D Coy 2 platoons in R. Works. 2 platoons in Reserve at Bn H.Q.? After 12 noon 16th A.1. A.2 Sectors were renamed Z.1 + Z.2. respectively and came under command of G.O.C. 95th Infty Bde. 95th Infty Bde. 18th French was handed over to Bn on our left. The left flank of 2 R.S.F. now rests on N. end of I.9 Trench.	A. B. S. R. T. Cambrai Sheet 1/40,000. Trench Map MARICOURT 1/10,000
	17-2-16		In Trenches. Quiet day & night. Some firing on our flanks. Trenches in a very bad state after recent bad weather. Coys employed in clearing & cleaning their trenches.	
	do			
	18-2-16		In Trenches. Relief of Coys took place. 2 platoons 2/Bedfords sent up to strengthen front line held by 2 R.S.F. as latter Coys were not strong enough to hold the line. Trenches much worse after continuous rain & thaw.	
	do			

WAR DIARY
or
INTELLIGENCE SUMMARY.
(Erase heading not required.)

Army Form C. 2118.

Place	Date	Hour	Summary of Events and Information	Remarks and references to Appendices
Trenches	19-2-16		In trenches. Bn detachment of 17th Manchesters in Z2 Subsection. Relief carried out by 17th C.O.R. Lieut Col Kennedy Jones from 3/R.S.F. and 2/Lt Godfrey rejoined from Base for duty. 1 Man Killed.	ALBERT pr-Contact Sheet 1/40,000. Trench Map MARICOURT 1/10,000.
SUZANNE	20-2-16		In trenches. Bn was relieved by 17th Manchesters in Z2 Subsection. Relief completed by 10.30 pm. Moved to SUZANNE into Bde Reserve in hmu R. Capt MJ McLean took over Command of D Coy.	
	21-2-16		In Billets. About 1 am hostile guns shelled SUZANNE. No casualties in R.S.F.	
do				
	22-2-16		In Billets in Bde Reserve. Batln several working parties, which took every available man.	
	23-2-16		In Billets in Bde Reserve. Bn moved into trenches which a new part of the line, which has become in Sect permanently. Dispos as follows: B Coy FARGNY MILL ½ C Coy " " R. Works 164. ½ C Coy " " ½ D Coy in BATTLE DUGOUTS. A Coy in billets in SUZANNE. ½ D Coy " " " " B.C. & ½ D Coy instr OC Z2 Subsectn for the present.	

WAR DIARY
or
INTELLIGENCE SUMMARY.
(Erase heading not required)

Army Form C. 2118.

Place	Date	Hour	Summary of Events and Information	Remarks and references to Appendices
	24-2-16		Part of Bn in trenches. Remainder in SUZANNE. 3 men hit in CROWS NEST (FARGNY MILL) from behind, probably by Battn now left.	ALBERT Contour Sheet 1/40000 Trench Map MARICOURT 1/10000
	25-2-16		As above. Relief of Coys took place commencing 6.30pm. Disposition as follows. A & ½ D Coy in FARGNY MILL. ½ C Coy in BATTLE DUGOUTS. ½ D Coy in R. Works (164) B & ½ C Coy in hutments SUZANNE. Hostile guns shelled SUZANNE intermittently from 3.30 - 10.30 pm. 1 Man slightly wounded.	
	26-2-16		As for 25th inst. Quiet day.	
	27-2-16		As above. Six Casualties occurred at FARGNY MILL by hostile snipers. 1 Man killed, 1 Man since died of wounds and 3 men wounded. Relief of Coys took place in the evening at 6pm. Bn disposed as follows. ½ A Coy in R. Works (164) ½ A Coy in FARGNY MILL. C Coy in FARGNY MILL. B Coy in BATTLE DUGOUTS. D Coy in huts SUZANNE. Message came about 9.30 pm "Gas 7th Div Centre". Considerable shelling actively South of R. SOMME in the evening. SUZANNE shelled in the evening.	

Army Form C. 2118.

WAR DIARY
or
INTELLIGENCE SUMMARY.
(Erase heading not required.)

Instructions regarding War Diaries and Intelligence Summaries are contained in F. S. Regs., Part II. and the Staff Manual respectively. Title pages will be prepared in manuscript.

Place	Date	Hour	Summary of Events and Information	Remarks and references to Appendices
Trenches	28-2-16		As fm 27th inst. 16th Manchesters on left. 18th Manchesters now Right. A few shells were fired into SUZANNE.	ALBERT Ordnance Sheet 57d-nw. Trench Map MARICOURT 1/10000.
	29-2-16		As fm 27th inst. Enemy shelled SUZANNE in the morning.	

C. E. Kembeck Major
Commanding, 2nd ROYAL SCOTS FUSILIERS

XXX (90). 7/30

2 R. Scots Fus.
Vol XVI

17.A.

Army Form C. 2118.

WAR DIARY
or
INTELLIGENCE SUMMARY.
(Erase heading not required.)

Instructions regarding War Diaries and Intelligence Summaries are contained in F. S. Regs., Part II. and the Staff Manual respectively. Title pages will be prepared in manuscript.

Place	Date	Hour	Summary of Events and Information	Remarks and references to Appendices
MARCH	1st 1916		Lt J. W. Towers Clark and 18 Other Ranks joined the Balln from 3/RSF. Relief of Coys took place commencing 6 p.m. Balln disposed as follows. B & D Coys FARGNY MILL, ½ C Coy R. Works 164. ½ C Coy BATTLE DUGOUTS. A Coy in HUTS SUZANNE	ALBERT confines Sheet 1/40000 French Map MARICOURT 1/10000
	2-3-16		Bn H.Qrs. move up to BATTLE DUGOUTS.	
	3-3-16		In trenches. Inspection made G.O.C. 90th Inf Bde. (names). RSF held Y2 Subsector consisting of FARGNY MILL, R. Works 164, BATTLE DUGOUTS, with 1 Coy in SUZANNE in Bde Reserve.	
	4-8-16		In trenches. Relief of Coys took place.	
	5.3.16		" " . 23 O.R. Lewis gunners joined from 3/R.S.F.	
	6.3.16		Very quiet day.	
	7-3-16		Quiet day	
	8-3-16		About 40 5.9" shells were fired into VAUX WOOD between 10+11 A.M. Considerable activity in the air throughout the day.	
	9-3-16		A few light shells were fired at working party at S. end of SUZANNE AVENUE when work was in progress.	
	10-3-16		VAUX WOOD & VILLAGE occasionally shelled but otherwise quiet	
	11-3-16		Quiet throughout the day but enemy artillery heavily shelled DUCKS POST & VAUX at dusk. S.O.S. DUCK POST sent out by 18TH MANCHESTERS in Y1 SECTOR at 7.30 P.M.	

Army Form C. 2118.

WAR DIARY
or
INTELLIGENCE SUMMARY.
(Erase heading not required.)

Instructions regarding War Diaries and Intelligence Summaries are contained in F.S. Regs., Part II. and the Staff Manual respectively. Title pages will be prepared in manuscript.

Place	Date	Hour	Summary of Events and Information	Remarks and references to Appendices
Y.2 SECTOR	11-3-16		2nd Bn. stood to. Considerable Machine Gun + Rifle Fire in the Marshes. Enemy captured KNOWLES POINT (G.S.C.73 VAUX).	Albert continued Mat 1/40,000
"	12-3-16		Quiet during the day but at dusk both sides shelled the Marshes round VAUX. Enemy ejected from KNOWLES POINT at 8.30 P.M. by 13th + 18th MANCHESTERS. Consolidated during early morning of 13th. 2/R.S.F. sent pack of our from ISLAND POST (A.29.D.3.3 VAUX)	Trench Map MARICOURT 1/10,000
"	13-3-16		A few shells fell near BATTLE DUGOUTS during the morning + some 5"9"'s on FARGNY MILL at 3.30 P.M. Considerable activity in the air observed in the morning by both sides. Several wounded Germans were seen crossing from BOATHOUSE to CURLU.	VAUX 62.C.N.N.3. 1/10,000.
"	14-3-16		Our aeroplanes were active though the afternoon. Aircraft reported to be large aeroplanes passed over VAUX at 8.45.P.M. followed by a heavy salvo on the MARSHES. About 9 P.M. MARICOURT was heavily shelled for a few minutes and SUZANNE + neighbourhood were shelled between 11 + midnight at times heavily. An officers patrol from ISLAND POST returned enemy working on a small ruined house about 20 yds from BRIDGE at A.29.D.5.0. (VAUX).	
	15-3-16		Quiet day. Relief plans took place.	
	16-3-16		Quiet day.	
	17-3-16		Quiet day.	
	18-3-16		About 1 a.m. hostile and our Artillery were active. Aeroplanes active in the morning. No hostile machines up. Quiet day.	
	19-3-16		Quiet day. Aeroplane active. Bn. relieved at 7 pm by 7th R.W. Kent Regt, 55th Inf.Bde, in Y.2 Sub-Sector. Relief Completed at 9.30 P.M. Coys, on Relief, marched independently to Camp at ETINEHEM. 9/K Inf. Bde in Divisional Reserve. 1 Man wounded before leaving trenches.	

Army Form C. 2118.

WAR DIARY
or
INTELLIGENCE SUMMARY.
(Erase heading not required.)

Instructions regarding War Diaries and Intelligence Summaries are contained in F. S. Regs., Part II. and the Staff Manual respectively. Title pages will be prepared in manuscript.

Place	Date	Hour	Summary of Events and Information	Remarks and references to Appendices
Camp Stenham done.	20-3-16		In Camp. 1 Shell was fired into STENHAM about 11 am. Calibre unknown, probably 8 in, no damage	ALBERT Contours Sheet 1/40,000
	21-3-16		In Camp. Draft of 50 other Ranks joined the Battn for duty from 3/RSF.	
	—do—			
	22-3-16		In Camp.	
	—do—			
	23-3-16		In Camp.	
	—do—			
	24-3-16		In Camp	
	—do—			
	25-3-16		In Camp. 2/Lt J.E. Gilkes joined the Battn for duty.	
	26-3-16		In Camp. Enemy dropped about 30 shells, 4.2 Calibre, about 400 yds from Camp, evidently searching for the Camp. No damage done.	
	—do—			
	27-3-16		In Camp. Enemy again sent a few shells over. Ration employed, while in Camp, on two permanent fatigues of 10 men + NCOs each. 50 men under 2/Lt D.D. Cormack at MERICOURT — Sun — Spring employed on unloading barges.	
	—do—			
	28-3-16		Bn marched to CORBIE at 10.30 am via main BRAY — CORBIE Road arriving at 2 pm. Distance 10 miles. One hostile shell fell near the Rear Coy (D) but did no damage. 17th KRR took over Camp from 2/RSF.	

Army Form C. 2118.

WAR DIARY
or
INTELLIGENCE SUMMARY.
(Erase heading not required.)

Instructions regarding War Diaries and Intelligence Summaries are contained in F. S. Regs., Part II. and the Staff Manual respectively. Title pages will be prepared in manuscript.

Place	Date	Hour	Summary of Events and Information	Remarks and references to Appendices
FLIXECOURT	29-3-16		Bn entrained at Pam for FLIXECOURT, arriving at LONGPRE Station at 10.15 am & FLIXECOURT at 1 pm. 2 platoons D Coy under 2/Lt S. Stewart sent to FREMONT for fatigue. H.Qr., B.C., D Coy at FLIXECOURT. A Coy at ARERRIBO for work under RE on Railway. H.Qr., B.C., D Coy at FLIXECOURT. Ration attached to 4th Army Infantry School for demonstrations. Lt Cain & Lt Harris took on charge B Grenade, Lewis Gun classes at the School.	Rep. AMIENS 2/Lt S. Stewart to FREMONT for fatigue. that 12 2/Lt S. Todd.
In Billets. FLIXECOURT.	30-3-16 -do-		In Billets. Batta. Employed on various duties. C Coy for demonstrations (attack etc) at 4th Army School. B Coy for ceremonial drill demonstrations. Small fatigue parties. ½ D Coy on permanent fatigue of 50 men under RE at 4th Army School.	
	31-3-16 -do-			

C.E. Lembrick Major
Comm.g 2nd R.S.F.

4/30

J R Scott Ins

Vol XVII

16-A
5 shuts

2nd R. Scots Fusiliers

WAR DIARY
or
INTELLIGENCE SUMMARY.
(Erase heading not required.)

Place	Date	Hour	Summary of Events and Information	Remarks and references to Appendices
APRIL				Reference AMIENS Sheet 12. 1/80000.
FLUXCOURT	1-4-16		In Billets	
	2-4-16		In Billets.	
	-do-			
	3-4-16		In Billets. 2/Lt W. N. Knox joined for duty from 3/R.S.F.	
	-do-			
	4-4-16		In Billets	
	-do-			
	5-4-16		In Billets	
	-do-			
	6-4-16		In Billets.	
	-do-			
	7-4-16		In Billets.	
	-do-			
	8-4-16		In Billets. B Coy demonstrates before Strissele Officers at 4th Army Infantry School in "Communic Drie". Regimental Transport, Bicycles and cookers inspected. Returned from the school in a pleasant.	
			In Billets. 2/Lt A.V. Morrison joined for duty from 9th R.S.F.	
	9-4-16			
	10-4-16		In Billets. Draft of 56 O.R. joined for duty from 3/R.S.F.	

Army Form C. 2118.

2nd R. Scots Fusiliers
CONFIDENTIAL
Date,
No.

WAR DIARY
or
INTELLIGENCE SUMMARY.
(Erase heading not required.)

Instructions regarding War Diaries and Intelligence Summaries are contained in F. S. Regs., Part II. and the Staff Manual respectively. Title pages will be prepared in manuscript.

Place	Date	Hour	Summary of Events and Information	Remarks and references to Appendices
FLIXECOURT	11-4-16		In Billets. C Coy demonstrated in attack before rest at 4th Army School.	AMSNS Sheet-12. 480,000
	12-4-16		In Billets.	
	do.			
	13-4-16		In Billets. D Coy demonstrates before "Commanding Officers" in "Ceremonial" Drill.	
	14-4-16		In Billets.	
	do.		In Billets.	
	15-4-16		In Billets.	
	do.		In Billets.	
	16-4-16		In Billets.	
	do.		In Billets. G.O.C. 90th Bde. inspects the Transport & Coys. at training.	
	17-4-16		Lecture &	
	do.		In Billets. Demonstration at 4th Army School by 30th Div. Grenade Schl. (Lt. D.H. Kennedy 2nd RSF)	
	18-4-16		In Billets. "Demonstration" at 4th Army School.	
			In "Bombers in the Attack".	
	19-4-16		In Billets. G.O.C. 90th Bde. inspects the Transport. Demonstration at 4th Army School	
			of "Smoke Bomb Gas, & Flammenwerfer".	

2nd R. Scots Fusiliers
CONFIDENTIAL Army Form C. 2118.
Date:
No.

WAR DIARY
or
INTELLIGENCE SUMMARY.
(Erase heading not required.)

Instructions regarding War Diaries and Intelligence Summaries are contained in F.S. Regs., Part II. and the Staff Manual respectively. Title pages will be prepared in manuscript.

Place	Date	Hour	Summary of Events and Information	Remarks and references to Appendices
FLIXECOURT	20-4-16		In Billets	Amiens Sheet 12. 1/80000 Amiens Sheet 17. 1/101,100
	21-4-16	do	In Billets.	
	22-4-16	do	In Billets. Demonstrations of various kinds at 4th Army School at which Army Corps Commanders were present. Demonstration in Bombing attack (attacq a September) by Lt Cair & 2 Bombers of D. Coy. Against Smoke attack, including bombs by the NCOs of the School.	
	23-4-16	do	In Billets. [illegible entries]	
	24-4-16	do	[illegible entries] In Billets.	
COISSY	25-4-16	do	Bn. less C Coy, marched to Coissy. Distance 15 miles at 10 a.m. Arriving in billets at 5 p.m. Dinners were taken "on the way". C Coy remained behind for a demonstration in the attack before the officers 4th Army School & were brought on by M.T. Arriving at 5 p.m. Major ?? Capt ?? ?? were in Battalion on proceeding.	
	26-4-16	do	In Billets Coissy.	

WAR DIARY or INTELLIGENCE SUMMARY

2nd R. Scots Fusiliers
CONFIDENTIAL

Army Form C. 2118.

Place	Date	Hour	Summary of Events and Information	Remarks and references to Appendices
	27-4-16 Consy		In Billets.	Ameins sheet 12. 1/80,000. Ameins Sheet 17. 1/100,000.
	28-4-16 –do–		In Billets.	
	29-4-16 –do–		In Billets. Battn parade in the morning. Several Officers NCOs & men attended demonstration of the "Stokes Gun" at XIIIᵗʰ Corps Trench Mortar School at POULAINVILLE.	
	30-4-16 –do–		Battn marches to CORBIE at 9am, via ALLONVILLE & DAOURS. Distance 10 miles. [illegible text] Br. arrives in billets at 3pm. Draft of 16 Other Ranks joins for duty from No.7 Infantry Base Depot.	

WAR DIARY
or
INTELLIGENCE SUMMARY.
(Erase heading not required.)

Instructions regarding War Diaries and Intelligence Summaries are contained in F.S. Regs., Part II. and the Staff Manual respectively. Title pages will be prepared in manuscript.

2nd R. Scots Fusiliers Form C. 2118.
CONFIDENTIAL
Date................
No.....................

Vol 18

Place	Date	Hour	Summary of Events and Information	Remarks and references to Appendices
May				Amiens Sheet 17 1/100,000
	1-5-16		Bn marched to BRAY at 3.30 pm. H.Q P.A & C Coys billeted in BRAY. B & D Coys at FROISSY (1½ miles South).	ALBERT Contour sheet 1/40,000
Trenches	2-5-16		Bn moved to trenches, took over Y2 Subsector from 7th R.W. Kents (55th Inf. Bde.) Relief complete at 7.30 pm.	French maps MARICOURT + VAUX 1/10,000
		at 11.15 pm	Bn disposed as follows: R.H. Coy hold 2 platoons FARGNY MILL & 2 platoons Q Works + RAVINE. L.H. Coy 2 Platoons A.29.4. "DANZIG ATE" + 2 platoons R Works + RAVINE. 2 Coys in SUZANNE, one in Batt Reserve and one in Batt. Reserve. Bn. HQ.? in RAVINE.	French Map MAURE PAS 1/20,000
	3-5-16		Day quiet. About 7.30 pm Enemy opened very heavy shell fire with 5.9" + 4.2 on A.29.4 + its vicinity. Slight damage done. No casualties.	
	4-5-16		Day quiet, occasional shelling. Hostile aeroplane brought down by our aircraft behind enemy's lines - fell in the marshes. At about 7-9 pm. Enemy sent up numerous coloured lights, no Verctin, however, could be made.	
	5-5-16		Enemy commenced a very heavy bombardment on French trenches South of R. SOMME. The French but a counter-barrage on German trenches assisted by our heavy guns. Bn stood to "Stand To". About 3.30 am, bombardment died down. No infantry action is reported to have taken place. From 4.15am to Stand down "Men" 3.30am Enemy shelled A.29.2 (12 Trench) at the Mill	19.A. 11 Whites

WAR DIARY
or
INTELLIGENCE SUMMARY.
(Erase heading not required.)

2nd R. Scots Fusiliers
CONFIDENTIAL Form C. 2118.

Instructions regarding War Diaries and Intelligence Summaries are contained in F.S. Regs., Part II. and the Staff Manual respectively. Title pages will be prepared in manuscript.

Place	Date	Hour	Summary of Events and Information	Remarks and references to Appendices
Trenches	5-5-16 (Cont)		Remainder of day quiet. Occasional shelling on both sides. Considerable activity in the air, chiefly British machines.	
	6-5-16		Quiet day. Enemy shelled A.29.4. Mill & Bn H.Q. with light shrapnel. Night was quiet.	
	7-5-16	-do-	Quiet day on the whole. Artillery on both sides fairly active. The Mill shelled with H.E. in the morning about 8am. About 60 shells in all. Several working parties Employed, chief work being deepening KIRBY AVENUE, pushing rear sap front of HdQrs Trench. 2/Lt. Gray joined on duty from the Cadet School	
	8-5-16		2/Lt. L.W.L. Lindsay - Young joined the Batln. for duty. Work was begun joining Saps 13 -19 together by using the Russian Sap method. [crossed out] Work on KIRBY AVENUE continued. Artillery fairly active.	
	9-5-16	-do-	Enemy artillery very active, chiefly against A.29.4 & the Mill. 13 Sap where tunnelling is in progress was blown in. About 100 4.2" Minenwerfers were fired round A.29.4 & its vicinity. Message received from Bde at 4pm that Germans knew possibly attack that night at 2am South of the R. SOMME. No attack took place. 1 Casualty. (wounded)	

WAR DIARY
or
INTELLIGENCE SUMMARY.
(Erase heading not required.)

2nd R. Scots Fusiliers
CONFIDENTIAL

Instructions regarding War Diaries and Intelligence Summaries are contained in F.S. Regs., Part II. and the Staff Manual respectively. Title pages will be prepared in manuscript.

Place	Date	Hour	Summary of Events and Information	Remarks and references to Appendices
Trenches	10-5-16		Our Artillery carried out two heavy bombardments against enemy's trenches in 43 Subsector & CHAPEAU de GENDARME, at noon & 2 p.m. respectively. Slack bombardment costs 1/4 hour. 2 men wounded.	Trench Map MARICOURT 1-VAUX 1/10,000
	11-5-16 do-		In trenches. Hostile Artillery active chiefly against A29.4 and also Fargny Mill. Some wire was put out in front of A29.4 Sap.	Trench Map MAUREPAS 1/20,000 MARICOURT
	12-5-16 do-		Artillery activity. Considerably less. After dusk, M.G. played at intervals on A29.4 Saphead & the wiring was being carried out.	MAUREPAS Short Contour Sheet 1/40,000
	13-5-16 do-		At 1 a.m. an intense bombardment of shells of all calibre was opened on A29.4 & the Mill. A hostile raiding party of about 2 NCOs & 12 men appeared at end of Sap A29.4 & followed the French & Artillery about half way up it but were then driven out by our men advancing to meet them, leaving 1 man killed in our trenches. Considerable confusion was caused at the commencement of the bombardment as a wiring party, listening patrol & miners were all at work at extreme end of Sap & were very nearly cut out by this bombardment. The enemy appear almost simultaneously with the opening of the bombardment. Their intention being to obtain prisoners, but this thing failed in doing against trenches held by the Battalion. Our Casualties were 2 killed, 12 wounded (3 since died of wounds) & 3 wounded shell shock at duty. The Battalion on our left, in 43 Subsector (18th Manchesters) were also attacked near Suzby forced into their trenches, about 6 men being missing.

WAR DIARY
or
INTELLIGENCE SUMMARY.
(Erase heading not required.)

Place	Date	Hour	Summary of Events and Information	Remarks and references to Appendices
Trenches	13-5-16		Communication by phone with front Coys broke down immediately. Main line to Bde H/Qrs was also cut but Communication with battn HQrs was maintained throughout. Battles on the flanks. Visual Signalling (lamp) proved very useful & was used as Alternative with front Coys. About 1.30 am information was received that 18th Manchesters in Y3 subsector were being attacked. 1 platoon of A Coy were sent to man the pivots in RONB AV which crossed the left flank of the Bn & would possibly be necessary the enemy from Comm Boyaux behind, had they broken through. This attack was however repulsed. "SOS" signal was sent through the phone on this Auth'y (A/149 Battery) put an effective barrage on enemy trenches. Rockets were a failure. Some patrols to left. The situation was normal by 3 am.	ALBERT Contour Shet 1/40,000. Trench Maps MARICOURT + VAUX 1/10,000. MAURSPAS Trench Map 1/20,000
do	14-5-16		Quiet day, practically no Arty activity. Night quiet.	
do	15-5-16		Day Quiet. Wiring was carried out in front of Sap A2q.9 which had been partly cut by hostile shelling in previous nine days.	
do	16-5-16		Enemy shelled FARGNY Mill & A.2q.q at intervals very heavily during this early morning & previous night. The Mill hitherto being badly damaged, apparently with the of making access to front trenches in this Sect difficult under observation. Night quiet.	
do	17-5-16		Quiet Day. Aeroplanes active in early morning.	

WAR DIARY or INTELLIGENCE SUMMARY

2nd R. Scots Fusiliers
CONFIDENTIAL

Place	Date	Hour	Summary of Events and Information	Remarks and references to Appendices
ALBERT Cambrai Trenches	17-5-16		Hohle Ashling has active. Several German Officers seen observing our lines near the PERONNE Road.	ALBERT Cambrai Sheet 1/40,000.
			Quiet night.	Trench Maps MARICOURT VAUX 1/10,000.
	18-5-16		Quiet day. Artillery very quiet.	
	19-5-16		Considerable aeroplane activity on our part. Party of 1 Officer & 40 men employed on Trench Mortar batteries. Bee Raisers Coy employed on Special Work under R.E.	Trench Map MARICOURT 1/20,000.
	20-5-16		Quiet day. Aeroplanes very active during the day. 2 hostile machines brought down behind our lines, one of them falling in J3 subsector. Machine completely wrecked & pilot burnt to death. Observer seen to fall out of the aeroplane. When found lying in "No Man's Land" near FARGNY Mill. Whilst men were to bring in the body but owing to machine gun fire at the point, it was not possible to bring him in.	Trench Map France 62° NW 1/20,000.
	21-5-16		A German machine gun in front of the aeroplane mentioned above was picked up near FARGNY Wood. Our Artillery carried out a heavy bombardment from just south of PERONNE Road to south end of J y front. Guns of all calibres up to 9 inch were firing. The 16 Bavarian Batteries bombarded CHAPEAU de GENDARME at the same time. Hohle Ashling near MARICOURT — SUZANNE valley was heavily shelled by 5/9 from 10-11 p.m. The body of German Observer mentioned above was brought in during the night. No papers were found on him. He was a Lieutenant of 11th & 87th Regt H.Q. 6 Division. Night quiet.	
	22-5-16		Quiet day. No shelling. Snipers more active.	
	23-5-16		Quiet day.	

2nd R. Scots Fusiliers
CONFIDENTIAL
Army Form C. 2118.
Date,
No.

WAR DIARY
or
INTELLIGENCE SUMMARY.
(Erase heading not required.)

Instructions regarding War Diaries and Intelligence Summaries are contained in F.S. Regs., Part II. and the Staff Manual respectively. Title pages will be prepared in manuscript.

Place	Date	Hour	Summary of Events and Information	Remarks and references to Appendices
ALBERT Trenches	24-5-16	—	Quiet day. No shelling.	ALBERT Contour Sheet 1/40,000.
	25-5-16	–do–	Quiet day. No shelling.	
	26-5-16	–do–	Quiet day. Aeroplanes active. Junction of 13 & 4 Saps attacked. Draft of 5 O.R. joined for duty from No. 7 Infantry Base Depot.	Trench Map MARICOURT & VAUX 1/10,000.
	27-5-16	–do–	Quiet day. Aeroplanes again active. Rev. Reeve C.F. (employed) on frostepping SUZANNE AVENUE.	Trench Map MARICOURT 1/20,000.
	28-5-16	–do–	As above. Draft of 4 O.R. joined from No. 7 Infantry Base Depot.	Trench Map France 62 C N 10 1/20,000
	29-5-16	–do–	Quiet day. Hostile aeroplanes more active than usual. One flew over our lines about 10.30 am flying low.	
	30-5-16	–do–	Quiet day. No shelling. 2nd Lt. G. Briggs joined for duty from 9th R.S.F.	
	31-5-16	–do–	Quiet day. Removed 9 stores prior to relief. Commenced.	

R. C. Walsh
LIEUT. COLONEL,
COMDG. 2nd ROYAL SCOTS FUSILIERS.

WAR DIARY
or
INTELLIGENCE SUMMARY.
(Erase heading not required.)

2 R Scots 2nd Vol 19

Place	Date	Hour	Summary of Events and Information	Remarks and references to Appendices
JUNE				
BRAY	1-6-16		In trenches. BSR handed over Y sectr to 37th Regt, 15th Division, French Army. RSF handed over 42 sector to 2nd Bn 37th Regt. Relief completed by 2:30 am. All stores SAA & grenades &c were taken out of the SecLR. Coys marched to BRAY, independently, after relief. Bn in Divisional Reserve. Battalion found the following working parties. 2 Coys at 7.30 pm each night under 205th Field Coy RE. 1 Coy ditto 9/25 thereabout. 1 Coy in Main position through the day. Work being carried out in dugouts at Cape & F trenches near ALBERT-BRONFAY Road near MARICOURT.	ALBERT Contour Sheet AMIENS Sheet 17. 1/40,000
	2-6-16		In Billets. Bn employed making paths under RE in town.	
	-do-			
	3-6-16		In Billets. as above. Draft 1.9 OR joined Bn today from No. 7 Inf Base Depot	
	-do-			
	4-6-16		In Billets. as above. The undermentioned Officer & NCOs have been awarded decorations for distinguished service in the Field. London Gazette dated 3/6/16.	
	-do-		Lieut W.L. Harris. Special Reserve. Military Cross	
			No. 12559 LCpl J. Dodd " "	
			9262 Cpl T. Hardman (Since Dis of Wounds) Military Medal	
			10242 LCpl A. Vincent " "	

WAR DIARY
or
INTELLIGENCE SUMMARY.
(Erase heading not required.)

Army Form C. 2118.

Place	Date	Hour	Summary of Events and Information	Remarks and references to Appendices
BRAY	5-6-16		In Billets. R.E working parties as above.	ALBERT Contours sheet 1/40,000
	6-6-16		In Billets. R.E working parties as above.	Amiens sheet 17. 1/40,000
	7-6-16	"	" " " " " " "	
	8-6-16	"	" " C.O. with G.O.C. 21st INF Bde visited the trenches in Z SECTOR. Coy Commanders, Lewis Guns Officer, Bombing Officer visited trenches in 22 SUB/SECTOR prior to taking over.	
	9-6-16	"	In Billets as above.	
	10 " "	"	" " "	
	11-6-16	"	In Billets as above. Bn. moved to trenches & took over 22 Sub-sector from 2ND WILTS R. 21st INF Bde. Relief completed by 1.30 AM. 13th disposed as follows:- Left Front B Coy Right Front D Coy. Supply A Coy Reserve C Coy + 2 platoons 17th MANCHESTER REGT owing to weakness of Coy strengths. These 2 platoons garrisoned U WORKS. 48 men employed under R.E. for special work. 30 men carrying party to miners digging Russian sap near the FLECHE (TALUS BOISÉ) Coys employed chiefly on cleaning and clearing trenches which were very muddy wet. Front Coys working day & night on NEW TRENCH N.4 of Quick.	

WAR DIARY
or
INTELLIGENCE SUMMARY

Army Form C. 2118.

Place	Date	Hour	Summary of Events and Information	Remarks and references to Appendices
Fauchez	12-6-16		Day quiet. Some shelling. A few aerial torpedoes fell near the FLECHE. No damage done. Night quiet. Working parties as before.	ALBERT continued Sheet 1/9000 AMIENS sheet 17 1/40000
	13-6-16		Many carrying parties during day. At 11.35 PM a very heavy bombardment was opened on our trenches from MARICOURT northwards and continued till 1AM. 8 Red Rockets was seen to go up on our Right + left flanks, accordingly S.O.S. ZZ was sent through to Bde + Batteries. Enemy attempted no raid on our front, but entered trenches occupied by the French in front of MARICOURT during 10 minutes. The Casualties in the Regt were 5 O.R. wounded. There was some delay in getting through 6 Battery but our barrage was very intense. Communication with Front Coy was cut at the outset, but a buried armoured cable kept communication with the Counter-attack Coy. Bombardment delay important work in progress which was resumed at 9AM.	
	14-6-16		In trenches. Working parties as before. 36 men carrying for Russian Saps. 2nd Lt NELSON wounded and admitted to 97th F.A. This Officer returned to light duty next day.	
	15-6-16		In trenches. Working parties as before. Officers 19th KING'S LIVERPOOL REGT visited the Rocks Blob to taking over. (Time put back one hour.)	

Army Form C. 2118.

WAR DIARY
or
INTELLIGENCE SUMMARY.
(Erase heading not required.)

Instructions regarding War Diaries and Intelligence Summaries are contained in F.S. Regs., Part II and the Staff Manual respectively. Title pages will be prepared in manuscript.

Place	Date	Hour	Summary of Events and Information	Remarks and references to Appendices
In trenches	16-6-16		In trenches. 2/Lt A.V. MORRISON wounded and admitted to 97th F.A. Work on NEW TRENCH almost completed.	ALBERT Contoured sheet 1/10,000 AMIENS SHEET 17. 1/40,000
do.	17-6-16		Working parties as before. Completion of 90th Bde relief by 19th Bde. 9th KING'S LIVERPOOL RGT. 19th relieved 2nd R.S.F. in Z.2 SECTOR	
	18-6-16		Relief quiet and completed by 130 a.m. Bn Marched by Coys to BOIS DE TAILLE all being up by 4 a.m. and breakfasted. Marched by Coys along Main BRAY-CORBIE Road to HEILLY arriving at 8 a.m. The transport had moved the previous night to CORBIE. Bn rested in a wood and entrained at 7 p.m. reaching AILLY-SUR-SOMME at 9 p.m. Detrained and marched to BRIQUEMESNIL arriving about midnight. Transport proceeded from CORBIE by road.	
BRIQUEMESNIL	19-6-16		Strong as possible Bn paraded at 9 a.m. arriving at theatre of operations at 9.15. 21st Bde attacked their trenches followed by 90th Brigade. Dinners were taken out. Returned to billets at 4.30 p.m.	
do	20-6-16		Capt + A/Adjt M/B BUCHANAN admitted to 98th F.A. and duties taken over by Lieut M. CARR. Bn paraded at assembly trenches on theatre with tools S.A.A. + stores and after training marched billets at 5 p.m. Marched to the open. @SHEET 1 commencing 30th Day.	
"	21-6-16		21st Bde moved forward + trenches. 98th Bde worked on the BM 7 p.m. 2nd Lieuts. R. KENNEDY + A.G. HENDERSON joined the BN	
	22-6-16		Bn paraded at 7.30 a.m. and marched to the theatre where two attacks were carried out under the C.O. The last time its attack was made on its own by N.C.O.s. Returned billets M. noon.	

WAR DIARY or INTELLIGENCE SUMMARY

Army Form C. 2118.

(Erase heading not required.)

Instructions regarding War Diaries and Intelligence Summaries are contained in F.S. Regs., Part II. and the Staff Manual respectively. Title pages will be prepared in manuscript.

Place	Date	Hour	Summary of Events and Information	Remarks and references to Appendices
BRIQUESMESNIL	23-6-16		Whole Brigade went over theater of operations finishing at 4 P.M. LT. LOMAX and 2/LT A.M. WHYTE from 6/7th Bn. joined for duty.	ALBERT Scrabbard sheet 1/9.000
do.	24-6-16		In the morning the Bn. attacked BRIQUESMESNIL for practice and in its afternoon went over the course, finishing at 4 P.M. 2/LT SLAUGHTER from 9th Bn joined.	AMIENS SHEET "7" 1/140,000
do.	25-6-16		The whole Brigade went over the course and Brigadier General addressed its Officers on the last hour before operations. The Brigade had a village-attacking and street fighting in BRIQUESMESNIL. Voluntary C.of.E. & C.of.S. parades. CAPT M.B.BUCHANAN joined from C.C.S.	
	26-6-16		Bn. paraded at 7.5. A.M. and marched via SPISSE-MONT & BREILLY to AILLY.SUR.SOMME where it entrained and left at 11.15 A.M. De-trained at MERICOURT at 12.30 P.M. and marched just beyond MORLANCOURT where half an hour's halt for lunch was had. Marched by Companies at 5.7 P.M. interval along BRAY-CORBIE road & through BOIS DE TAILLY to Camp No. 2 ETINEHEM arriving between 4+5 P.M. Great activity by French and British Artillery. Draft of 149 O.R from 6/7th. 13th & GORDOCK joined the 13th.	
ETINEHEM	27-6-16		In Camp. British & French Artillery extremely active.	
	28-6-16 do.		In camp. Artillery activity continues.	
	29-6-16 do.		In camp. Working parties of 12 men from each Coy. proceed to ASSEMBLY Trenches for work prior to being occupied.	
	30-6-16 do.		Working party 1/1 NCO + 12 men working on ASSEMBLY TRENCHES. Bn. moves out in 2 Columns to ASSEMBLY Trenches at 7.P.M. and 7.40 P.M. Coy 3. Div inspected Camp at 9.30.am	

War Diary

of

2nd Bn. Royal Scots. Fusiliers.

for

July 1916.

WAR DIARY or INTELLIGENCE SUMMARY

Army Form C. 2118.
2 R.S. Fus.
90 Bde
2/30
In Succ Fusiliers
CONFIDENTIAL
Vol 2
July
20 A
13 sheets

Place	Date	Hour	Summary of Events and Information	Remarks and references to Appendices
ASSEMBLY TRENCHES	1-7-16		The Bn. Manned its Assembly Trenches between midnight and 1 A.M. having left ETINEHEM CAMP ALBERT MAP in two halves at 6.10 + 7.10 P.M. (30-6-16) and joined the rest of the Brigade (which moved from BILLON WOOD) in two parallel columns. Only waterproof sheets + rations for one day - besides emergency ration - were carried and on each man's back was a yellow patch. 30TH DIV. - and a metal disc. Every man - with exception of bombers. who carried 10 - carried 2 No.5 grenades and 200 shovels, 100 picks + a quantity of sandbags were distributed over the Bn.	AMIENS (S.17) 1/40,000 MONTAUBAN 1/20,000
		7.30 A.M.	Zero War fixed for 7.30 A.M. and an intensive bombardment started apparently at 5 A.M. The Bn. left its trenches and CAMBRIDGE COPSE at 8.30 A.M. in the following order:- Three platoons of NETTOYEURS from B,C+D Coys. - marked by yellow shoulder strap - behind	
		8.30 A.M.	the third waves of 16TH MANCHESTERS on the left + 17TH MANCHESTERS on the right. The remainder of the Bn. moved in two lines of columns of half platoons - 150 yards between Coys. - C + B Coys on right + A + D on left - with its right on the W. end of GLATZ REDOUBT and its left on TALUS BOISÉ. There was very little shell-fire and hardly any casualties occurred before reaching BRITISH Front Line - 1000 yds. - After reaching the German lines this Bn. considerable rifle fire from the left flank which decreased as the Bn. advanced causing numerous casualties in A + D Coys. The 18TH DIV. who were operating W. of the TALUS BOISÉ appeared to be held up and to be keeping to the trenches while the enemy could be plainly observed firing on our own. The Bn. however kept its formation perfectly.	
		9.20 A.M.	The Bn. halted in conformation with the leading Bns. the Bde. having covered the ground too quickly, the barrage being on MONTAUBAN till 9.55 A.M. Owing to the mass of shell craters the ground was difficult to manoeuvre over but no trouble was experienced from enemy fire.	

WAR DIARY
or
INTELLIGENCE SUMMARY.
(Erase heading not required.)

Army Form C. 2118.

2nd R. Scots Fusiliers
CONFIDENTIAL

Instructions regarding War Diaries and Intelligence Summaries are contained in F.S. Regs. Part II and the Staff Manual respectively. Title pages will be prepared in manuscript.

Place	Date	Hour	Summary of Events and Information	Remarks and references to Appendices
MONTAUBAN	1.7.16	9.30 A.M.	The Bde moved again but halted at 9.45 A.M. when the advance seemed to waver. The barrage lifted off the village and both B & C Coys caught up the 17TH MANCHESTERS. A + D the 16TH MANCHESTERS on the right + left desperately about 400 yards from the village. Our field guns again put a barrage on the village.	ALBERT Combined Scale 1/ AMIENS (St.7) 1/40,000 MONTAUBAN 1/20,000
		10 A.M.	The whole Bde advanced again on NETTOYEUR platoons + most of the Bn being in the consulting line. There was no rifle fire from the village itself but it was still heavy from the left flank.	
		10.15 A.M.	A Coy had reached the Sunken Keep and the remaining other Coys had occupied the trench S. of the village. (SOUTH TRENCH) by 10.30 A.M. and the whole started consolidating. The casualties during the advance were: OFFICERS: Killed LIEUT J.W. TOWERS-CLARK (Comdg A Coy). 2ND LT. T.H.L. GRIERSON (C Coy). Wounded; CAPT & ADJT M.B. BUCHANAN. CAPT. M.J.N. LAW (O.C. D Coy). LT. J.S. CRAIG (A Coy). 2LT A.G. LOCHHEAD (D Coy). W.M. KNOX (C Coy). CAPT. G.D. FAIRLEY R.A.M.C. att. Total 8. O.R. Killed 18. Wounded 94. Missing 58. Total 170. Only 20 Officers had been taken into action + Fighting strength was 743 O.R. LT COL. R.K. WALSH Comdg 2/R.S.F. had been previously invalided. O.C. MONTAUBAN. The Adjt duties were taken over by LT M. CARR. All strong points and trenches so far as recognisable were occupied as practised but touch was not obtained with the 18TH DIV. on the left. The NETTOYEUR platoons after clearing the village rejoined their Coys. One platoon taking 28 prisoners. Several batches of prisoners including an Artillery Brigadier and his staff were conducted to the rear. The Bn was disposed as follows. A Coy holding KEEPA. One Platoon of D Coy/ust S. in KEEP E, Rest of D Coy W end of SOUTH TRENCH, BN. HD QRS, C, Coy + B Coy	

Army Form C. 2118.

WAR DIARY
or
INTELLIGENCE SUMMARY.
(Erase heading not required)

Instructions regarding War Diaries and Intelligence Summaries are contained in F.S. Regs., Part II. and the Staff Manual respectively. Title pages will be prepared in manuscript.

Place	Date	Hour	Summary of Events and Information	Remarks and references to Appendices
MONTAUBAN	1.7.16		at E. end of SOUTH TRENCH. The 16TH + 17TH MANCHESTERS holding MONTAUBAN ALLEY – trench N. of the village – with the N/neuve(?) and the E. perimeter of the village respectively. Trench with 21ST BDE. in CHIMNEY TRENCH was established.	ALBERT Contoured Sheet 1/40,000 AMIENS (57.17) 1/40,000 MONTAUBAN 1/20,000
		12 noon	The enemy continued putting heavy shrapnel over KEEP A and this with the shortage of tools seriously held up the work of consolidation.	
		12.30 PM	Enemy guns turned their attention to other parts of the village and heavy enfilade fire from S.9. + 4.2's was brought to bear on NORD + TRAIN ALLEYS. The carrying parties of MANCHESTERS which had been stationed at A KEEP now returned to obtain more stores from forward Bde. Dump.	
		2.45 PM	One platoon of C.Coy was sent to reinforce KEEP B, held by 17TH 17, which was being heavily shelled. The remaining two companies of the 18TH MANCHESTERS had previously moved into SOUTH TRENCH – their H.Q. adjacent to those of 2/R.S.F. to screen from the garrison.	
		5 PM	D Coy's platoon was withdrawn from front E owing to the heavy and continuous shell fire and the impossibility of consolidating that position.	
		8 PM	Enemy shelling increased and continued throughout the night gun fire in the direction of BERNAFAY WOOD enfilading SOUTH TRENCH causing several casualties. One of our own batteries was also putting shells into the village.	
		10.30 PM	One platoon of B Coy was moved to NORD ALLEY to NORD ALLEY where it remained by the continual shell fire.	
"	2.7.16	2 AM	Another platoon of B Coy was moved to the ORCHARD + not being required immediately, remained in TRAIN STREET. The Whole BN was ordered to stand to at 2 AM.	
		3 AM	Contradictory reports were received from the front two Bns. as to the Germans attacking and in response to a call for reinforcements 2 platoons of D Coy. + the whole	

WAR DIARY or INTELLIGENCE SUMMARY

2nd R. Scots Army Form C. 2118.
CONFIDENTIAL

Place	Date	Hour	Summary of Events and Information	Remarks and references to Appendices
MONTAUBAN	2.7.16		of C Coy was moved up to re-inforce the 16TH MANCHESTERS in MONTAUBAN ALLEY and our platoon was employed in bombing out the enemy who had four casualties — left a few as prisoners. The enemy having lodged himself in a straight length of trench it was found to be impossible to move him.	HEBERT (Courbusset Sheet) 1/40,000 AMIENS (5H7) 1/40,000 MONTAUBAN 1/20,000
		6 A.M.	2ND WILTS (21ST BDE) relieved 16TH MANCHESTERS and our Coy in KEEPA, which withdrew to SOUTH TRENCH. The 18TH MANCHESTERS were ordered to withdraw to the railway RAVINE and hold themselves in readiness for counter-attack while immediate reinforcements were to be found by 2/R.S.F. Signalling had been carried on so far mostly by visual from S. of the village. Enemy shelled the village throughout the day & bomb was very difficult.	
		6 P.M.	Enemy commenced a heavy bombardment with ten shells in the direction of MARICOURT-MONTAUBAN. Guides having been hurriedly dispatched to Bde H.Q. the enemy's gunnists began to arrive.	
		10 P.M.	The middle of the relief Bde reported S.O.S. so having been sent out but no attack was apparent. Relief was continually held up and our artillery put a very heavy barrage round the village. 17TH MANCHESTERS signalled themselves to weak that B Coy were moved to take over the whole of NORD ALLEY from CHIMNEY TRENCH to CENTRE of CAFÉ-TRÉ HOUR village	
"	3.7.16	3 A.M.	Relief of 2 R.S.F. by 12TH ROYAL SCOTS (9TH DIV) completed and the BN marched by small units to HAPPY VALLEY and bivouaced with the rest of the Bde. Additional officer casualties:- Missing believed killed 2ND LT. Y. GODFREY (BDE LEWIS MG party) Wounded L⁺ F.G. GRIFFITHS (B Coy) CAPT. P.W.T. MCGREGOR-WHITTON (C⁺ Coy) Making a total of 11 OFFICERS. O.R. Kill. A 38 W198 M.50. Total 286. L⁺ POTTER R.A.M.C. attached vice FAIRLEY All officers made good so far as possible. Day spent in resting the men. G.O.C. 90TH INF Bde addressed the Regt. Heavy thunderstorm at 4 P.M.	
HAPPY VALLEY	4.7.16			

Army Form C. 2118.

2nd R. Scots Fusiliers

WAR DIARY
or
INTELLIGENCE SUMMARY.
(Erase heading not required.)

Instructions regarding War Diaries and Intelligence Summaries are contained in F. S. Regs., Part II. and the Staff Manual respectively. Title pages will be prepared in manuscript.

Place	Date	Hour	Summary of Events and Information	Remarks and references to Appendices
HAPPY VALLEY	5.7.16 6.7.16		G.O.C. again addressed the Bn. Very wet and uncomfortable day for the men. Physical Training + Route Marches to Battery Post BRAY. D Coy found burying party of 2 officers 16 N.C.Os + 100 men for work on the battlefield. 1st Bn was at VAUX SUR. SOMME. Draft of 59. O.R. joined the Bn.	ALBERT (Contoured sheet) 1/40,000 AMIENS (5K17) 1/40,000 MONTAUBAN 1/20,000
	7.7.16		Parades as before. 1st Bn arrived at BRONFAY FARM (3rd Div). C Coy found party as above for burying. Draft of 117 O.R. from depot + base joined the Bn.	
	8.7.16 10 A.M.		Orders received to be ready to move at half-an-hour's notice. S.A.A. grenades were drawn & issued as far as possible — complete except for our Coy — and Coys marched off independently	
		1.20 P.M.	via BRONFAY FARM — PERONNE RD — to GIBSON ST. a trench just N. of CAMBRIDGE COPSE — where the Bn settled in at 6 P.M. and rations were drawn and regimental tools were too used & be carried on the men. At 10 P.M. C.Os went to Bde. Hd. Qr.	
		10.30 P.M.	Bn was ordered to move to VALLEY SUPPORT TRENCH which it did, by Coys across the open — the whole Bde. moving forward. These orders were altered half-way across + Bn was now ordered to move to TRAIN ALLEY with its head at Bde H.Q. at GLATZ REDOUBT, a move which took considerable time.	
	9.7.16	12.15 A.M.	Our guide lost provided to guide the whole Bn to the BRIQUETERIE. In the darkness and the shelling the Coys lost touch & this was considerable confusion but the greater part of the Bn were in the SUNKEN ROAD running from the BRIQUETERIE to MALT HORN TRENCH. by 3 A.M.	
		3 A.M.	Attack postponed till 5.30. A.M.	
			Disposition of Bn was as follows. B Coy supported by D Coy in MALT HORN TRENCH to attack the FARM and C Coy lined the N. face of the trench preparatory to attacking the trench running from the S.E. corner of TRONES WOOD	
		5.30 A.M.	A preliminary bombardment of 40 minutes and at 5.30 the Coys attacked.	

WAR DIARY or INTELLIGENCE SUMMARY

Army Form C. 2118.

Place	Date	Hour	Summary of Events and Information	Remarks and references to Appendices
MALT HORN TRENCH	9.7.16	5.30 AM	MALT HORN FARM was captured with but little opposition — only 2 O.R. Casualties, our prisoners being captured. The other objective was also reached in short time. But there was considerable grenade fighting in the pits. 109 prisoners & 2 Machine guns were captured by C. Coy (Capt P.W.T. McGREGOR-WHITTON (O.C. Coy) was killed and there were several casualties among O.R. The whole enemy trench was occupied as well as the STRONG POINT at XXXXXXX junction of GUILLEMONT RD & TRONES WOOD) but touch was not obtained with the 17TH MANCHESTERS who were supposed to be advancing through TRONES WOOD but apparently did not attack for some hours afterwards. Nor did the French Regt. on our right move as had been promised. Consolidation started at once and more S.A.A, grenades, tools & stores were brought up. Enemy commenced shelling the open ground S. of the woods & also the FARM. The French put out a post to watch the right flank of the trench dug W. of the Farm but which could not be joined up with the trenches on its flanks. A bombing post was established in the Farm.	ALBERT Trench Map 1/40,000 AMIENS 5k 7 1/40,000 MONTAUBAN 1/20,000
		7 AM	Trench was at last established with the 17TH MANCHESTER R. in TRONES WOOD and they were asked to take over the STRONG POINT.	
		10 AM	One Coy of 2ND WILTS was allowed to assist in holding the line. One Coy of 2ND WILTS was allowed to assist in holding the line. B.N. H.Q. with others from the front line to the BRIQUETERIE had by this time become very active heavily shelling TRONES WOOD & our trenches at times badly enfilading them. One Coy of 18TH MANCHESTER R. from TRONES WOOD relieved the Coy of WILTS in our line. The 17TH MANCHESTER R. appear to have withdrawn about this time from TRONES WOOD	

WAR DIARY
or
INTELLIGENCE SUMMARY.

(Erase heading not required.)

Army Form C. 2118.

Place	Date	Hour	Summary of Events and Information	Remarks and references to Appendices
MALT HORN TRENCH	9.7.16		This exposure of our left flank necessitated the withdrawal of our Coy from its strong POINT. Some 300 yds down the trench where a block was made. 2nd Lieut T.W. NELSON being wounded. All our Coy without any officers which was relieved by officers being transferred from other Coys. Throughout the day the shelling was very heavy and there was considerable doubt as to the exact position in TRONES WOOD.	19 ON 7.11.16 AM 1/24,000
		4.30 PM	The enemy attacked from the direction of ARROW HEAD COPSE but were driven off our trenches with heavy losses from the French artillery and our rifle fire, though it was found they had re-occupied the part of the trench running from TRONES WOOD to our bombing post. At dusk two Coys of the 16TH MANCHESTER R dug in along SW edge of the TRONES WOOD and pushed their patrols into the wood & one Coy of the 19TH MANCHESTER R. which had remained there all day withdrew. This left the whole of TRONES WOOD in the enemy's hands and their rifle & machine gun fire badly enfiladed C Cy. Heavy shelling by the enemy's 5.9"s + 4.2"s continued throughout the night but there was no further infantry attack. D Cy relieved B Coy in MALT-HORN FARM with 2½ platoons, B Cy having been under continual shell fire since 10 A.M in the morning. Ration parties had to be sent back as far as the GLATZ REDOUBT which was exceedingly difficult to attain. Touch with the 16TH M R at S.W. Corner of TRONES WOOD was kept during the night by patrol.	
—11—	10.7.16	6.40AM	There was a very heavy bombardment of our trenches in the early morning. Some bombing was heard in TRONES WOOD and enemy were reported to be working along the SOUTHERN EDGE. 2nd Lt R KENNEDY severely wounded — later died of wounds. 2nd	

WAR DIARY
or
INTELLIGENCE SUMMARY.
(Erase heading not required.)

Army Form C. 2118.

Instructions regarding War Diaries and Intelligence Summaries are contained in F. S. Regs., Part II. and the Staff Manual respectively. Title pages will be prepared in manuscript.

Place	Date	Hour	Summary of Events and Information	Remarks and references to Appendices
MALT HORN FARM.	10-7-16		Enemy snipers exploding his trench. Enemy artillery was much less active throughout the day but there were intermittent bursts of heavy shelling. During the evening our guns continued shelling TRONES WOOD with shrapnel and at 10 P.M. 17TH K.R.R. were seen to attack the WOOD & were later seen to return with some 4TH SOUTH AFRICAN SCOTTISH who had been in trench just S.W. of the WOOD. Our Lewis Guns had been co-operating in this attack by firing on the E face of TRONES WOOD and the GUILLEMONT RD.	MONTAUBAN 1/20,000 ALBERT 1/40,000 contoured sheet
		10.30 P.M.	Ration guides were dispatched to the junction of the BRIQUETERIE RD + the OLD GERMAN FRONT LINE when they met the relieving regiment the 20TH K.L.R. Relief was complete at 1 A.M.	
	11.7.16	1 A.M.	BN. marched by small units to MARICOURT and occupied its defences. Rations were drawn + rum issued. The remaining regiments of the Bde, who were reported as having heavy casualties also withdrew to MARICOURT.	
		3 P.M.	Casualties during these operations 2/R.S.F. were :- OFFICERS Km 1, 2. W.2 . OR. 93. After heavy shells fell in MARICOURT Our artillery very active during the day.	
		4 P.M.	BN was relieved by the 8TH EAST SURREY REGT and marched with a distance of 150* between platoons to BRONFAY FARM.	
		6 P.M.	BN closed at BRONFAY FARM and marched via the loop N. of BRAY + BRAY-CORBIE Rd to BOIS CELESTINS arriving at 9.30 P.M. 2ND LT. LINDSAY-YOUNG returned from Base hospital. Three drafts, 52 - 59 + 21 (H.L.I) OR joined the BN.	
BOIS CELESTINS	12-7-16		Resting + cleaning up.	
"	13-7-16		Corps Commander addressed the BN just prior to marching off stating that the 30TH Div. had	

Army Form C. 2118.

WAR DIARY
or
INTELLIGENCE SUMMARY.
(Erase heading not required.)

Place	Date	Hour	Summary of Events and Information	Remarks and references to Appendices
	13-7-16		Bn now passed under the orders of the 2nd CORPS. and congratulating the Regt. on its performance	ALBERT Combined Shut 1/40,000. SOMME VALLEY ROAD AMIENS (M.1) Combined Shut 1/40,000.
		12.10PM	Bn paraded at 12.10 P.M. and marched at the head of Bde. via BAILLY LAURETTE - SOMME VALLEY ROAD - CORBIE to DAOURS where the whole Bde. was billeted at 6 P.M.	
DAOURS	14-7-16		Day spent in resting and cleaning up. Draft of 38. O.R. joined the Bn.	
" "	15-7-16	10.30.	Divisional General addressed the 90th Inf. Bde. and afterwards inspected the newly arrived drafts. Draft of 35. O.R. from Base depôt joined the Bn.	
" "	16-7-16		C. of S. parade at 11 o'clock - Col. E. at 11.30 A.M. All officers attended at Bde. H.Q. at 6.30 P.M. drawn from the recent fighting was discussed.	
			2nd LT W.L. HAY appointed Bn. L.G.O. and LT W.L. HARRIS to command C.Coy. + 2/Lt H.L. ATKINS A Coy.	
		7PM 9AM	Bn. went route march to LAMOTTE In afternoon work was carried out under Coy arrangements. Classes for instruction in Lewis Guns + bomb throwing were commenced. Following awards by C. in C. appeared in Special memo. to appear in gazette in due course.—	
			No. 8979 C.S.M. T. MILLER Military Cross	
			No. 8915 C.S.M. H. ETHERIDGE Military Cross	
	18-7-16		Col. paraded. D.W. General went round billets and inspected two of the Coys. Sgt. Majors parade in afternoon.	
	19-7-16	10. AM	Orders received that Brigade would move during the morning. Bn. was out on a route march + had to be recalled. Bn. paraded at 1.30. PM and marched at the head of the Brigade via LANEUVILLE - CORBIE to BOIS CELESTINS arriving at 7.P.M after a trying hot + trying march	

Army Form C. 2118.

WAR DIARY
or
INTELLIGENCE SUMMARY.
(Erase heading not required.)

Instructions regarding War Diaries and Intelligence Summaries are contained in F.S. Regs., Part II. and the Staff Manual respectively. Title pages will be prepared in manuscript.

Place	Date	Hour	Summary of Events and Information	Remarks and references to Appendices
	20.7.16			ALBERT (Combined Sheet) 1/40,000 MONTAUBAN 1/20,000
HAPPYVALLEY	21.7.16	7.15 A.M.	B[n]. paraded at 7.15 A.M. and marched with Bde to HAPPY VALLEY arriving at 10.30 A.M. Envoy shelled BRAY. 2nd LT A.V. MORRISON (reported) + 38 O.R. joined the B[n] for duty. Coy heads. Several German aeroplanes over our lines being heavily shelled by our A.A. guns. The following Officers joined the B[n]. LT. R.D. PATON, R.A.G. TAYLOR, 2LT. R.H. ASHTON, R.M. THORBURN, M.W. KENNEDY, J. McA. GRACIE, P.M. HUGH, G.B. DUNCAN, D.P. IRVING + W. SMALL, 21st W.I.M. YOUNG, W.G. SHEPPARD	
	22.7.16		Coy paraded in morning. The whole B[n] moved at 4 P.M. with 100X distance between platoons to area occupied by 21st Bde just W. of CARNOY	
	23.7.16		The B[n] 6 Officers and 200 details remained with Transport and Stores at HAPPY VALLEY. The Bde. was in support to the 21st Bde. who was attacking GUILLEMONT	
		9.30 P.M.	The B[n] moved with the rest of the Bde through CARNOY to trenches round CAMBRIDGE COPSE Enemy intermittently shelled CARNOY valley. Howsons + ANZACS. 2nd LT. W. NELSON "MILITARY CROSS".	
	24.7.16	6 A.M.	Orders received at 6 A.M. for the Bde. to move N. of the old German line + hold line which the B[n] did over the open by platoons occupying VALLEY TRENCH, ALT TRENCH, TRAIN ALLEY. B[n] H.Q. in a joined fortsound in some cave affording little cover. Orders were proposed for the continuous shelling of area occupied by the B[n] with 8 + 5.9 inch shells, owing at our battery us, but causing 30 casualties. Patrol returned bringing useful information. Remaining patrols of Bde. did not get out owing to gas shells.	
	25.7.16		B[n] left its trenches, dumping overcoats + stores, + moved back by platoons + coys. W. of CARNOY to trenches attack on GUILLEMONT. Orders received to remain in present position. Orders were brought down by transport.	
	26.7.16			
	27.7.16		Several enemy aeroplanes flew unmolested over our lines. B[n]. moved back in the evening to area just N. of the Citadel (F.21.d.5.8.)	

Army Form C. 2118.

WAR DIARY
or
INTELLIGENCE SUMMARY.
(Erase heading not required.)

Instructions regarding War Diaries and Intelligence Summaries are contained in F.S. Regs, Part II. and the Staff Manual respectively. Title pages will be prepared in manuscript.

Place	Date	Hour	Summary of Events and Information	Remarks and references to Appendices
CARNOY	28.7.16		Short route marches by Coy. in morning. Great activity in the air on both sides.	ALBERT (Contoured Sheet) 1/40,000. MONTAUBAN 1/20,000
	29.7.16	9.30 A.M.	The Bn. MARCHED — with the rest of the Bde. — moved by half platoons at 200x distance to SILESIA TRENCH + SUPPORT. Whilst tools & stores were drawn + everything got ready for action. Details, stores + transport moved to area occupied by the Bn.	
	30.7.16	12.15 A.M.	Bn. continued moving forward by platoons from SILESIA TRENCH. The enemy was making use of gas shells which necessitated the wearing of helmets going along MARICOURT-MONTAUBAN Rd. The MALTZ HORN TRENCH was very much congested with troops. The Assembly trenches just E. of TRONES WOOD and running N+S of the TRONES WOOD – GUILLEMONT ROAD were reached about 3.30 A.M. The Bn. suffered very few casualties getting into position. Bn. H.Q. was established in tunnel under TRONES WOOD – GUILLEMONT RD. but no telephone wires to Bde. H.Q. could be found. The Bn. was disposed as follows. A+B Coys. in his dug running N+S on south side of GUILLEMONT – TRONES WOOD Rd. with A Coy in front. D Coy. was in trench N. of road + C Coy for want of any new/safe/and trench as planned were in a trench running parallel to the road.	
		4.45 A.M.	Zero was fixed at 4.45 A.M. There were movable barrages across its whole age at 0.8, 0.15, 0.20, 0.40 + 0.65. The Bn. went forward in lines of half companies on a frontage of 260 yards at 60x distance. One (platoon) from each Coy. acting as Nettoyeur of which two platoons were in its 2nd line + two in the third line. Lewis guns went up behind the 4th line. There was a heavy mist at the time of advance. The enemy put a barrage about TRONES WOOD but there was little rifle fire at the time of the commencement. Bn. H.Q. was to move forward with two companies of 16TH MANCHESTERS who were in close support but never appeared. O.C. 2 W.R.S.F. had been previously appointed Commandant of GUILLEMONT	

WAR DIARY
or
INTELLIGENCE SUMMARY

Army Form C. 2118.

Place	Date	Hour	Summary of Events and Information	Remarks and references to Appendices
	30-7-16		One Coy of 17TH MANCHESTER R. who were to have occupied trenches vacated by the Bn afterwards and was immediately sent forward to support the attack which from reports received appeared to be hung up in places. Communication with the advance was kept by runner but on the mist clearing this became exceedingly difficult message taking from two to three hours to get from the village. A second Coy of 17TH MANCHESTER R. appeared much later and in view of the situation was ordered to hold the line of trenches through ARROW HEAD COPSE. About our hour after zero two officers of the 16TH MANCHESTER R. reached Bn HQ & stated that their men had been pretty broken retired. From further reports received it appeared that while the 19th had reached its objectives both E & W of GUILLEMONT the advance on both flanks had failed. Orders were sent to O.C. D Coy which was the nearest Coy to get into touch with the remaining Coys & form the best possible defensive line but these orders never reached their destination. The remaining Coys were ordered to conform.	ALBERT (Continued Sheet) 1/40,000 MONTAUBAN 1/20,000
		10.AM	By this time the enemy had put a very heavy barrage along the E face of TRONES WOOD and the mist having completely cleared and the road & intervening ground swept by Machine Guns communication became practically impossible. It had been impracticable to obtain any communication with even the advanced H.Q. of Bn and only runners therefore could be used.	
		11.noon	LT MORRAN, O.C. D Coy reached Bn HQ having been sent from the village by a Capt. of the 18TH MANCHESTER Regt to report on the situation. He stated he had fought his way through the village & knew the 19th could not be cut off.	
			It now appeared that the advance of the 89TH Bde had failed and that they were practically occupying their original line. The Bn was completely isolated. It was impossible to withdraw owing to the exposed nature of the ground. Later a F.O.O. reported that he had recd about 300 Hun surrender on the left. The Bn went into action 20 officers + 750 O.R. strong. Of these only 3 officers + about 40 O.R. — chiefly H.Q. Staff—remained under the Colonels Command. About 100 O.R. reformed later having made their way back through the 89TH Bde	

WAR DIARY or INTELLIGENCE SUMMARY

Army Form C. 2118.

2nd R. Scots Fusiliers
CONFIDENTIAL

Place	Date	Hour	Summary of Events and Information	Remarks and references to Appendices
ALBERT (Contalmaison) 1/40,000 MONTAUBAN 1/20,000	30.7.16		CASUALTIES: OFFICERS. Kin.A: 2/Lt. H.L. ATKINS, 2/Lt G.H.W. BLACKMAN. Wounded: 2/Lt A.V. MORRISON, A.G. HENDERSON, R.D. PATON, W.M. KENNEDY + H.T. KENNEDY (remained at duty) Missing: Lts. C.N.J. KENNEDY, W.S. ADMAX, 2ND LTS. G.H. SLAUGHTER, R. H. ASHTON, P.McHUGH, G.B. DUNCAN. Wounded + Missing: LT W.L. HARRIS, 2/Lt D.P. IRVING, J.M. McA. GRACIE + W. SMALL. Total. 17	
			O.R. Kin.A: 15 Wounded: 40 Missing: 578 Total 633 TOTAL 650	
			Remnants of the Btn. under O.C. 2/R.S.F. held the line E. of TRONES WOOD but owing to unsteadiness of its troops and uncertainty of the position in TRONES WOOD the situation was precarious. The enemy heavily shelled the line of trench round Bn. H.Q. + TRONES WOOD throughout the day.	
		9.30 PM	A heavy burst of shelling caused the MANCHESTER R. to evacuate ARROW HEAD COPSE while two other Coys who had returned to their BN. H.Q. behind TRONES WOOD stating their trenches were untenable were reported as being sent back but were apparently allowed. The enemy made no counter attack as had been expected.	
	31.7.16	2 A.M.	Reinforcements of 2 Coys. H.L.I. arrived and manned the Rd. to the R.w.	
		4 A.M.	The leading Coy. of the 8TH KINGS LIVERPOOLS arrived and after handing over its line in accordance with instructions, received Bn. H.Q. moved back to ground W. of CARNOY arriving about 8 A.M.	

R.L. Wale
LIEUT: COLONEL
COMDG. 2nd ROYAL SCOTS FUSILIERS

90th Brigade.
30th Division.

2nd BATTALION

ROYAL SCOTS FUSILIERS

AUGUST 1 9 1 6

WAR DIARY or INTELLIGENCE SUMMARY

2nd R. Scots Fus. Army Form C. 2118. CONFIDENTIAL

Place	Date	Hour	Summary of Events and Information	Remarks and references to Appendices
HAPPY VALLEY	1-8-16	—	Men rested. Divl General addressed the Bn.	ALBERT (captured sheet)
	2-8-16	—	Bn paraded at 3.45.A.M. and marched at the head of Brigade via MORLANCOURT + TREUX to MERICOURT arriving at 8.30.A.M. Entrained at 11.30. on supply train and went via AMIENS to LONG PRÉ. LES. CORPS SAINTS detraining at 6.30 P.M. Transport leaving the previous night successful by road.	1/40,000 SHEET. 36.A. 1/40,000
LONGPRE	3-8-16	—	Resting + cleaning up.	
	4-8-16	—	Bn paraded at 5.30 P.M. and marched to LONGPRE STATION + entrained leaving at 6.41 P.M. going via ABBEVILLE FREVENT ST POL. to BERGUETTE	BETHUNE Combined Sheet Ed. 6. 1/40,000.
BERGUETTE	5-8-16	—	Bn detrained at BERGUETTE at 4.30. A.M. and marched via GUARBECQUE + BUSNES to L'ECLEME arriving in billets at 8 A.M. Divn formed part of XI TH CORPS	
L'ECLEME	6-8-16	—	Cof E. + C. of S. Parade.	
do	7-8-16	—	In billets. Route March, Bathing + handling of arms etc.	
do	8-8-16	—	" "	
do	9-8-16	—	" "	
	10-8-16	—	Bn paraded at 1.15. P.M. and marched to LA MICQUELLERIE when the Bn was inspected by General HAKING Commanding 1ST ARMY returning to billets by 4. P.M.	
	11-8-16	—	Bn paraded at 5.10 A.M. and marched at the head of Bn from L'ECLEME via BUSNETTES + CHOQUES to BETHUNE standing (the day outside the town) and arriving in billets at ECOLE DES JEUNES FILLES at 7 P.M. CAPT. STAVERS (6/7TH BN) joined the Bn.	
BETHUNE	12-8-16	—	Coy Parades. Bombing + Lewis Gun classes continued.	
	13-8-16	—	Church Parades in morning. Enemy put about 5-9" shells into BETHUNE about 4 P.M.	
	14-8-16	—	Parades as usual. Firing on range	
	15-8-16	—	" "	
	16-8-16	—	" " Enemy put about 16 shells of varying size into the town between 1+4 P.M.	

WAR DIARY
or
INTELLIGENCE SUMMARY
(Erase heading not required.)

Army Form C. 2118.

2nd R. Scots Fus. CONFIDENTIAL

Instructions regarding War Diaries and Intelligence Summaries are contained in F. S. Regs., Part II. and the Staff Manual respectively. Title Pages will be prepared in manuscript.

Place	Date	Hour	Summary of Events and Information	Remarks and references to Appendices
BETHUNE	17-8-16	—	Coy Parades as before.	BETHUNE Combined rial 1/40,000
"	18-8-16	—	" " " in "C" BRANCH. T/LT. WRIGHT joined Bn for duty. 2LT AM WHITE attached to 21ST INF. BDE. as Bomber	
"	19-9-16	—	1 Officer & 150 O.R. employed from 8 A.M. to noon digging Cable trench in GIVENCHY SECTOR BETHUNE shelled with light shells during afternoon. 2LT G.G. COGHILL joined for duty & 2LT W.M. SYFRET admitted 16.F.A.	
"	20-9-16	—	Church Parades. Party of N.C.O.s & 20 men for instruction in Trench Duties. Coy Wksp in order A.B.C.D. Tour in trenches 72 hours.	
"	21-8-16	—	1 Officer & 150 OR for Cable trench. Enemy shelled BETHUNE.	
"	22-8-16	—	Parades as usual. BETHUNE Shelled. 2 LT SYFRET rejoined from F.A.	
"	23-8-16	—	" " "	
"	24-8-16	—	Cable digging working party and 38 O.R. for loading at ANNEZIN.	
"	25-8-16	—	Parades as usual. 2LTs J.S. ALLAN & R.C. COONEY joined Bn for duty. BETHUNE Shelled.	
"	26-8-16	—	Working parties as above. BETHUNE Shelled during the night.	
"	27-8-16	—	" " "	
"	28-8-16	—	" " "	
"	29-8-16	—	LT. COL. WALSH took command of Company and of 90TH INF Bde. Holcomb & Ayards. Pte IRVINE & T. GOURLEY & T. CHURCH B.S.M. MAS MACDONALD S. & WILLIAMSON ? Shot to O Feeder redeemed wounded Around & shelled lute BETHUNE 4 woken 1 + 3 A.M. Company parades musketry on range	
"	30-8-16	—	" Shelled BETHUNE at 1, 2 + 4 A.M. Parades as usual.	
"	31-9-16	—	G.O.C. 30TH Div. inspected the Bn. at 10 A.M.	

C.S. Kimbell Major for LIEUT: COLONEL,
COMDG. 2nd ROYAL SCOTS FUSILIERS.

SECRET.   Volume. 3.

WAR DIARY.

For the month of September 1916.

2nd Battalion Royal Scots Fusiliers.

                                            Lieut Colonel.
1-10-16.   Commanding 2nd Bn Royal Scots Fusiliers.

WAR DIARY or INTELLIGENCE SUMMARY

Army Form C. 2118.

(Erase heading not required.)

Instructions regarding War Diaries and Intelligence Summaries are contained in F. S. Regs., Part II. and the Staff Manual respectively. Title Pages will be prepared in manuscript.

Place	Date	Hour	Summary of Events and Information	Remarks and references to Appendices
BETHUNE	1-9-16	—	Enemy shelled BETHUNE at 1.44 A.M. B'n route march & drill.	BETHUNE (contd.shed) 1/40,000 FESTUBERT TRENCH MAP
"	2-9-16	—	Work under Coy arrangement. Lt. Col. R.K. WALSH resumed command of B'n.	
"	3-9-16	—	Church parade. 90th Bde. relieved 93rd Inf Bde. 2nd R.S.F. relieved 16th & 18th W. YORKS in VILLAGE LINE – RUE DE L'EPINETTE. FESTUBERT – LE PLANTIN. C Coy. B'n BETHUNE 9 p.m. & took over billets of posts. Rest of B'n relieved during afternoon. Remainder of B'n marched at 7.30 P.M. Trench Sketch 372. Relief completed by 10.30 P.M. Transport at LES FACONS. CAPT STAVERS admitted to F.A.	
Trenches	4-9-16	—	Very quiet night. Coys employed repairing existing keeps.	
"	5-9-16	—	Quiet both night & day. Work on KEEPS continued.	
"	6-9-16	—	Our guns fairly active. Enemy very quiet.	
"	7-9-16	—	" " " "	
"	8-9-16	—	Work on KEEPS continued. Enemy fired a few light shells close to FESTOS FM about 4.30 P.M. 2nd R.S.F. relieved 17th Bn MANCH REGT in Mallar FESTUBERT sector. 16th Bn MANCH took over VILLAGE LINE. Relief of FESTUBERT carried by day. Relief of B'n. Completed 11 P.M. Total Trench Sketch 327. B'n disposed as follows. A Coy Left Front. B Right Front. D Close Support in COVER TRENCH C in SUPPORT in RICHMOND TERRACE. One Coy of 17th MANCHESTERS attacked to O.B. in Reserve. Front line consisted of series of Island Posts. Trenches quite shallow and breastworks are very low & weak in places. Night quiet. Lewis guns fired on places where enemy was known had been cut.	
"	9-9-16	—	Stokes guns fired from COVER TRENCH intermittently during the day. About 3.30 P.M. enemy commenced shelling Island Posts & COVER TRENCH with 77mm + 10cm. Evidently searching for T.M. Batteries. About 90 shells fell in all causing temporary evacuation of one or two Islands. Casualties. Officers K'd A 2nd Lt. W.M. YOUNG. O.R. K'd A3 W. 13 CAPT W.M. STAVERS wounded B'n from F.A. Following Officers from 9th B'n posted for duty. 2nd Lts. G.H. GRICK, G.S. MACKAY, J.H. CAMPBELL, D.B. MACKENZIE, A.H. GREEAR, W.J. MERRY, F.W. FRANCIS, + A. KING.	

WAR DIARY
or
INTELLIGENCE SUMMARY

Army Form C. 2118.

(Erase heading not required.)

Place	Date	Hour	Summary of Events and Information	Remarks and references to Appendices
Trenches	9-9-16	—	One (1) platoon back to left + Right Front Coy, left COVER TRENCH to relieve casualties. One platoon moved from Res. Coy to RICHMOND TERRACE.	BETHUNE (Contoured Sheet) 1/40,000
"	10-9-16	—	Enemy quiet during night except for Machine Gun Fire. Damage to Island + Sandwork repaired as far as possible. Enemy artillery very quiet throughout the day. Work on parapet + wire continued. Casualties. 1 O.R. wounded.	FESTUBERT TRENCH MAP.
"	11-9-16	—	Enemy quiet both night + day. 12 Rifle Grenades fell near right front Coy. In "C" company relief commencing at 8.30.P.M. + complete at 11 P.M. Casualties 2 O.R. wounded. HONOURS + AWARDS. D.S.O. Lt. Col. R.K.WALSH. MILITARY CROSS. CAPT. J. MURRAY, 2/Lt H.T.LAWDON (att. 21st Bde M.G. Coy.) 2ND LT D.D.CORMACK. D.C.M. No. 18575 L.Cpl. F. KNAGGS. No. 9290 Cpl. A. MANTLE. MILITARY MEDAL.	AMIENS SHEET 12.
"	12-9-16	—	Quiet except for Machine gun fire on both sides. Three hostile working parties dispersed.	
"	13-9-16	—	Quiet night except for MG fire. Two hostile working parties dispersed. Very quiet during the day. A few Right Trench Mortar rounds fell between COVER TRENCH + RICHMOND TERRACE. 1 O.R. wounded.	
"	14-9-16	—	Machine guns active during the night. One hostile aeroplane approached our lines but was driven off by our A.A. guns. No hostile shelling during the day. 2nd R.S.F. relieved by 18th + 13th MANCH R. Bn. moved into billets at LE TOURET. Relief complete by 10.30 P.M.	
LE TOURET	15-9-16	—	Resting and cleaning up. Hostile aeroplane over LE TOURET in evening. Draft of 128 O.R. joined Bn.	
"	16-9-16	—	Sudden orders for move received. 325 O.R. on working party recalled. Bn. left LE TOURET heading goes to 147th YORKS + LANCS at 2.45.P.M. + settled into billets at ESSARS by 4.15.P.M.	
ESSARS.	17-9-16	—	Bn. paraded at 12 noon + marched via BETHUNE to billets at MONT BERNENCHON arriving 2.P.M.	
MT. BERNENCHON	18-9-16	—	Transport moved at 12 noon + Bn. paraded at 2.30 P.M. + marched via GONNEHEM to CHOCQUES for entraining. Train at 5.P.M. via Hpool DOULLENS to CANDAS. Bn. detrained at 7.30 P.M. and	

Army Form C. 2118.

WAR DIARY
or
INTELLIGENCE SUMMARY
(Erase heading not required.)

Instructions regarding War Diaries and Intelligence Summaries are contained in F. S. Regs., Part II. and the Staff Manual respectively. Title Pages will be prepared in manuscript.

Place	Date	Hour	Summary of Events and Information	Remarks and references to Appendices
BEAUVAL	18.9.16	—	Marched to billets at BEUVAL about 3 miles.	AMIENS SHEET 12.
— " —	19.9.16	—	Resting + cleaning up. Draft of 15 O.R. joined in July. Capt H. MILES 2/R.SF awarded Military Medal.	
— " —	20.9.16	—	Bn. Route March at 9.30 A.M. Company work in afternoon.	
— " —	21.9.16	—	Bn. paraded at 7.50 A.M. and marched in the rear of the Brigade via TALMAS + VILLERS-BOCAGE to FLESSELLES, where 90th Brigade was billeted arriving at 11.30 A.M. Owing to lack of billets Bn. did not arrive down till 6 P.M. Draft of 139. O.R (2/5th H.L.I.) joined the Bn.	
FLESSELLES	22.9.16	—	Physical Training + Company Parades in morning. Bn. paraded at 8 P.M. + took part in Night Operations advancing over open ground and digging in on reaching objective.	
— " —	23.9.16	—	Company work in morning. Night operations at 8 P.M.	
— " —	24.9.16	—	Church Parade in morning.	
— " —	25.9.16	—	Bn. paraded at 8.45 A.M.	
— " —	26.9.16	—	Company parades. Tests with Intensive + wire intensive digging practice carried out. Bn. paraded at 4.30 A.M. and carried out an attack at dawn with remainder of Brigade returning to billets at 1 P.M.	
— " —	27.9.16	—	Bn. paraded at 4.30 A.M. and carried out an attack at dawn with remainder of Brigade. Returned to billets at 9 A.M.	
— " —	28.9.16	—	Company + Specialist Training. 2.Lt. S.H. FROST admitted to F.A.	
— " —	30.9.16	—	do. do. 2.Lt. S.H. FROST admitted to F.A.	

R. Welch
LIEUT: COLONEL,
COMDG. 2nd ROYAL SCOTS FUSILIERS.

VOLUME 3.

S E C R E T.

W A R   D I A R Y.

For the month of October 1916.

2nd Bn Royal Scots Fusiliers.

                                    Lieut Colonel.
2-11-16.   Commanding 2nd Bn Royal Scots Fusiliers.

WAR DIARY or INTELLIGENCE SUMMARY

Army Form C. 2118.

Place	Date	Hour	Summary of Events and Information	Remarks and references to Appendices
FLESSELLES	1.10.16	—	Church Parade at 10 + 10.30 A.M. After C of E. Parade Bde. formed up on ground E. of FLESSELLES and Divisional Commander presented Medal Ribbons.	AMIENS SHEET 17 & 62 D. N.E. 1/20,000 5/c. S.W. 1/20,000
" "	2.10.16	—	Brigade Operation from 9 A.M. to 1 P.M.	
" "	3.10.16	—	Company work. Transport moved with Brigade from FLESSELLES STN. at 3 P.M. to CARDONETTE.	
" "	4.10.16	—	B.N. paraded at 9.20 A.M. and en-bused on French buses on VIGNACOURT-FLESSELLES RD. with remainder of Div. Brigade moved off at 11.30 A.M. and went via VIGNACOURT- ST VAAST- AMIENS- QUERRIEU to DERNANCOURT from where Brigade marched to billets at BUIRE arriving at 5.30 P.M.	
" "	5.10.16	—	Work under Coy. arrangements.	
" "	6.10.16	—	B.N. paraded at 5.15 P.M. and marched in rear of Brigade via cross-country tracks + MEAULTE to camp just W. of FRICOURT arriving about 7 P.M.	
" "	7.10.16	—	Physical Training + Bayonet Fighting. Draft of 29 O Ranks joined B.N. 2Lt W.M. M. FREITAG joined	
" "	8.10.16	—	Work as above. Bde under orders to move at 4 hours notice.	
" "	9.10.16	—	Draft of 5 NCO's joined for duty	
" "	10.10.16	—	B.N. paraded at 5.55 A.M. and marched just N of the head of 90th Brigade via MAMETZ and MONTAUBAN to ground just N. of the Alter where the whole Division. Bombs, tools + rockets where issued + great coats and haversacks were collected. The B.N. carried the rations for the following day from ration parties + water-proof sheet in the pack. The B.N. moved off by Coys at 4 P.M. + marched to LONGUEVAL where it met guides of the 10th Queens and 32nd R. FUS. 41st Division — and went via FISHALLEY + TURK LANE taking over lines at N. 19. a 4. B.N. was 20 Officers + 450 O.R. strong the remainder, about 200, staying with the Transport. B.N. was disposed as follows:- Left Front Coy. B Right Front Coy A. In Intermediate Support - C. Gird Support Trench D Coy. BN / H.Q. in old German dug-out in GIRD TRENCH	

WAR DIARY
or
INTELLIGENCE SUMMARY
(Erase heading not required.)

Army Form C. 2118.

Place	Date	Hour	Summary of Events and Information	Remarks and references to Appendices
Trenches	10-10-16	—	2ND BEDFORDS. 89TH BDE. was on the left - 7TH BN. NORFOLK R. on the right - 12TH DIV. 21ST Brigade were in Divisional Reserve. Bde. H.Q. were just S. of FLERS. Communication over such a distance necessitated a chain of runners being established between this point and H.Q. of BNS.	5/C.S.W. 1/20,000.
— » —	11-11-16	—	Relief of 10TH QUEENS & 32ND FUS. was completed at 1.30.A.M. The day was spent in improving and deepening trenches. Bombardment of hostile lines commenced at 7AM. to which enemy replied intermittently and inaccurately at 3.15 P.M. Our heavy shells - 6. inch - were continually dropping short (as they continued to do throughout the operations) & Bn's front in the line falling often in rear of the GIRD SUPPORT LINE These "shorts" were responsible for two Officers Casualties and about 40. O.R. Many suffering from Shell Shock. Bombardment at a slacker rate from 5 P.M. throughout the night. The greatest difficulty was experienced in getting up rations, water & stores owing to the distance & men losing their way.	
— » —	12-11-16	—	Bn. was ordered to be in position for assault by dawn. and a Coy of the 18TH MANCHESTERS which was to accompany the BN in the attack arrived in GIRD SUPPORT as well as a Nettopen Platoon of the same regiment which joined C Coy The 17TH BN MANCHESTER R. having relieved 2ND BEDFORD R. was now on the BN's left Zero was fixed at 2.5 P.M. from which time a series of creeping barrages were to carry BN's to their second objective - a line of trenches about 300 yards from our front lines The BN as ordered went forward in four waves: - 1st wave A Coy. on the right. B Coy on the left with the right of A Coy just E. of the FLERS-LIGNY RD. and the left of B Coy on the track running N&S though N.9.a. central. 2nd & 3rd waves C & D Coy. the former having the Nettopen platoon of 18TH MANCHESTER R. divided 4TH wave D Coy. 18TH MANCHESTER REGT.	

WAR DIARY or INTELLIGENCE SUMMARY

Army Form C. 2118.

Place	Date	Hour	Summary of Events and Information	Remarks and references to Appendices
Trenches	12.10.16	—	The attack was at once met by considerable Machine Gun & Rifle Fire and a barrage of Artillery barrage. The enemy field of view and undamaged by our bombardment from accounts received the attack was held up about 100x from its 1st objective. A similar late met the Units on the Bn's right & left. All telephonic communication from the Commencement of the attack and the intensity of the enemy's fire made it impossible to obtain any news. Quickly two orderlies sent forward by Bn H.Q. returned with a report that the attack had collapsed, which was confirmed later by the return of two officers. Steps were taken to re-organise the Bn in the original hour line. At dusk several wounded returned when fresh shell holes in front of our parapet. Among the 20 Officers & 450 O.R. who went into action there were the following casualties:- OFFICERS:- K.in A. Lieut J.R.D. McEWEN 2/Lts. J.S. ALLAN & T.H. BOYLE. WOUNDED. 2/Lts. W.M. SYFRET, A.L. MACKAY, A.H. CRERAR, Q.S. MACKAY, W.G. SHEPPER C.G. COGHILL. O.R.- K.in A. 40. WOUNDED 147. MISSING 27. Shell Shock 47. TOTAL:- OFFICERS 9. O.R. 261. The night was spent in re-organizing and repairing the trenches & evacuation of casualties. The 2ND R.Scots.Fus. & 18TH MANCHESTERS held the right sector of the Brigade.	57C S.W. 1/20,000
"	13.10.16	—	The night was fairly quiet. Consolidation continued. About 6 P.M. S.O.S. was sent up in error by the Regt. on our Left which caused heavy artillery fire from both sides. Enemy used gas shell through the night. Partial relief of Bn by details from the Transport. Those relieved went to FLERS SUPPORT.	
"	14.10.16	—	Relief complete by 2 A.M. The night & early morning were quiet. There was continuous	

Army Form C. 2118.

WAR DIARY
or
INTELLIGENCE SUMMARY

(Erase heading not required.)

Instructions regarding War Diaries and Intelligence Summaries are contained in F. S. Regs., Part II. and the Staff Manual respectively. Title Pages will be prepared in manuscript.

Place	Date	Hour	Summary of Events and Information	Remarks and references to Appendices
Trenches	14.10.16	—	Artillery fire throughout the day, becoming intense at 1 P.M. and between 4 & 5 P.M. During the evening the 19th MANCHESTERS were withdrawn from the sector, except those in GIRD SUPPORT + their Lewis Guns.	57 C.S.W. 1/20,000
"	15.10.16	—	Enemy heavily bombarded our lines at 3 A.M. and again at 5 A.M. causing a few casualties. Apart from this the day was quiet. Commencing about 8 P.M. the remainder of the BN was relieved by the 17th MANCHESTERS. Enemy was very quiet during relief which was complete about 10 P.M. the BN joining up with the party in FLERS SUPPORT.	
"	16.10.16	—	89th Bde + 21st Bn Regiment relieved 90th Brigade. At 4 P.M. after having guides for incoming units the BN moved from trenches in parties of 30 strong via TURK LANE + LONGUEVAL to W. of MONTAUBAN where it went into tents. Bivouacs arriving at 9 P.M. 2 Lts J.B. ORR + J. McLEOD joined the BN for duty from 4/5th BN.	
"	17.10.16	—	Day was spent in cleaning up, checking rolls + making good deficiencies. 50 O.R. employed in road making.	
"	18.10.16	—	BN was under orders to move at one hours notice the Brigade being in Divisional Reserve. 1 Officer + 30 O.R. took charge of Prisoners Cage relieving party of 29th Division.	
"	19.10.16	—	Heavy rain prevented any work.	
"	20.10.16	—	BN employed in work on roads.	
"	21.10.16	—	"	
"	22.10.16	—	BN paraded at 7.30 A.M. and marched at the head of 90th Brigade via MAMETZ – MEAULTE – DERNANCOURT – BUIRE – to billets in RIBEMONT arriving at 12 noon. Strength 12.5 OR (14th H.L.I.) + 52 OR (12th R. Scots) joined the BN. The following Officers joined from 4/5th BN. 2 Lts R.D. SMITH, D. TRENCH, J.K. MORRAN, J.S. CAMPBELL, J. MELVILLE, J.C. CAMPBELL, D. FRASER, J.T. FRASER, A.H. CHAMBERS, J.B. EDGAR.	
RIBEMONT	23.10.16	—	Cleaning up + kit inspection.	
"	24.10.16	—	Coy parades.	
"	25.10.16	—	"	

WAR DIARY or INTELLIGENCE SUMMARY

Army Form C. 2118.

(Erase heading not required.)

Place	Date	Hour	Summary of Events and Information	Remarks and references to Appendices
RIBEMONT	26.10.16	—	Bn paraded at 9 AM and marched to MERICOURT STATION where it entrained in a supply train leaving at 12.30 P.M. Route via CORBIE – AMIENS – FLESSELLES – CANAPLES to DOULLENS where Bn detrained at 9.30 P.M. & billeted. 30th Division passed into III Army.	LENS SHEET 11 51 e SW 1/10,000
DOULLENS	27.10.16	—	Bn paraded at 9 AM and marched via GROUCHES – LOUCHEUX to billets at WARLUZEL arriving at 12.30 P.M.	
WARLUZEL	28.10.16	—	Coy Parades. Reconnaissance of New Area.	
" – "	29.10.16	—	Bn Church Parade. 90th Brigade commenced relieving 139th Brigade (46th Div) Bn marched via COUTURELLE – SAULTY – BAC DU SUD to billets at BAILLEULVAL arriving at 6 P.M. Bn was in Divisional Reserve. Strength of Coys about 150 O.R.	
BAILLEUVAL	30.10.16	—	Bn moved off by platoons commencing at 11 A.M. & marched via BASSEUX – BIENVILLERS & relieved 6th Bn SHERWOOD FORESTERS in Right Sector of Bde Front. Relief complete by 2 P.M. Disposition of Bn was as follows. Left Front. 14 Coy. Centre Front 13 Coy. Right Front D Coy Reserve (billets GROSVILLE) C Coy. Bn H.Q. in GROSVILLE. Enemy very quiet. Draft of 70 O.R. joined	
Trenches	31.10.16	—	All available men employed in clearing falls in the trenches caused by heavy rain. A few light shrapnel fell on Centre Sector. 1 O.R. Wounded.	

VOLUME 3.

SECRET.

WAR DIARY

FOR THE MONTH OF NOVEMBER 1916.

2nd Battalion Royal Scots Fusiliers.

3-12-16.

Major.
Commanding 2nd Bn Royal Scots Fusiliers.

WAR DIARY or INTELLIGENCE SUMMARY

Army Form C. 2118.

(Erase heading not required.)

Place	Date	Hour	Summary of Events and Information	Remarks and references to Appendices
TRENCHES	1-11-16	—	Artillery on both sides very quiet. All three men of Reserve Coy employed under R.E. Enemy raid Patrol did not encounter the enemy. Our artillery carried out intermittent bombardment between 7 P.M and Major McConaghey joined as 2nd in Command. Enemy fired 12.77mm shells behind GROSVILLE at 1.30 P.M. Our artillery was quiet. Station very quiet.	65/C.S.W.F. 1/20,000
" —	2-11-16	—	Draft of H.O.R. joined for duty. Work as about. Our Artillery + T.M.s bombarded enemy lines from 1 P.M – 2.30 P.M. Slight enemy retaliation damaged trench of rig N/Port Coy. Lieut Chapman joined as Transport Officer.	
" —	3-11-16	—	Resting, clearing of falls, + wiring. Enemy very quiet.	
" —	4-11-16	—	Work continued. A few light shells fell on GROSVILLE + Support line during the day.	
" —	5-11-16	—		
" —	6-11-16	—	Bn relieved by 17th/3rd MANCHESTER REGT. Lewis gun relief commenced at 9 A.M. + companies at 10 A.M. Relief complete by 12.30 P.M. Bn moved into Brigade Reserve Billets at BELLACOURT. One Coy occupied line of posts along BELLACOURT-BRETENCOURT Rd. Garrison one Platoon + one Lewis gun in each Post. 2 N.C.O.s + 30 men for R.E. Working Party.	
BELLACOURT	7-11-16	—	8 N.C.O.s + 240 men on R.E. Working parties at 8.30 A.M. Evening parties cancelled owing to heavy rain. The following officers joined for duty from FORT MATILDA 2/Lieuts G. DICEY, W. LINDSAY, A.T. MAYES, F. ROBB, H.F. SMITH, J. GILCHRIST. R.E. Working Parties – 300 hours.	
" —	8-11-16	—	Intermittent bombardment of enemy lines from 7.30 to 11.30 P.M.	
" —	9-11-16	—	Our Coy on R.E. Work. Remaining Coys rested.	
" —	10-11-16	—	2nd R.Sc Fus relieved 17th Bn MANCHESTER R. in the right subsector. Commencing at 8.30 A.M. Relief complete 6.12 noon. Dispositions of 13th A. & D. Coys in front line. B Coy in reserve. Work continued under R.E. Front line to be cleared except for Lewis Gunners + sentries every 100x, in trenches under R.E.	
" —	11-11-16	—	Front on the 13th Bn + 30th Div. front about 1000x to the right. Forma pros. for liberation of gas on 13th Div.	
" —	12-11-16	a.m.	sent off about 2 a.m. Work continued. 30th Div. 745.	

WAR DIARY or INTELLIGENCE SUMMARY

Army Form C. 2118.

Place	Date	Hour	Summary of Events and Information	Remarks and references to Appendices
Trenches	12.11.16	—	No retaliation on our front	O.I.C. S.E. 1/20,000
"	13.11.16	—	R.E. work continued. Trench cleared by 5 P.M. for liberation of 12"TH DIV" Gas which commenced at 5.30 P.M. and ended about 8 P.M. At 6.30 P.M. twelve light shrapnel burst over the left front Coy.	
"	14.11.16	—	Work as above. A few light shells fell on various parts of the sector during the day. Patrol at night did not encounter the enemy.	
"	15.11.16	—	Work as above. About 40 medium trench mortars fell about R.32.d doing no damage	
"	16.11.16	—	Informant light shelling of our front doing no damage. Much enemy transport heard + trains. Heard behind enemy lines. Feu 1 A.M.	
"	17.11.16	—	Work as above. Aircraft now active in the morning. Enemy's artillery was very quiet.	
"	18.11.16	—	17TH BN MANCHESTER REGT. relieved 2ND R. Sc. Fus. in right sub-sector. Relief completed by 12 noon. B.N. HD. QRS. Lewis Guns + BG. Coys. were billeted at BAILLEUVAL + CD. Coys at BASSEUX. B.N. in divisional reserve.	
BAILLEUVAL / BASSEUX	19.11.16	—	Church parades in morning. Kit inspections + bathing. Enemy put about 250 + 5" into BAILLEUVAL between 9 + 10 P.M.	
"	20.11.16	—	Company parades.	
"	21.11.16	—	" " MAJOR W.L CAMPBELL joined for duty	
"	22.11.16	—	" "	
"	23.11.16	—	C.O's kit inspection. 1 Officer + 20 O.R. on carrying work at BEHACOURT	
"	24.11.16	—	2ND R. Sc. Fus. relieved 17TH BN MANCHESTER REGT. in right sub-sector. Relief completed 12.30 P.M. Telk. milled shelling by enemy	
Trenches	25.11.16	—	Quiet night. All available men employed with R.E. superintendence. Honours + Awards SGT. J MCINTYRE "MILITARY MEDAL"	
"	26.11.16	—	Work as before. Artillery very quiet	
"	27.11.16	—	" " 12 Heavy trench mortars fell on right front Coy's line doing some damage and causing our casualty about 4 P.M. Trench mortar emplacement was shelled. 2/LT T.W NELSON reported	
"	28.11.16	—	Work as usual. Quiet night. Gas trench mortars bombarded hostile lines in front of BLAIRVILLE WOOD. Machine gun levis guns coöperated. 5.30 P.M. GAS ALERT ON.	

WAR DIARY
or
INTELLIGENCE SUMMARY
(Erase heading not required.)

Army Form C. 2118.

Place	Date	Hour	Summary of Events and Information	Remarks and references to Appendices
Rivelon	29.11.16	—	Quiet night - Misty morning. Germans, including an officer, seen near our wire were fired on about 10.15 A.M. Big working parties were sent out during the night & our patrols were active but did not succeed in finding the enemy.	51.C.3.E 1/20,000
— " —	30.11.16	—	17th 13th MANCHESTER REGT relieved 2/R.S.F in Right Sub Sector commencing at 9 A.M relief complete by 12.30 P.M. A Coy. held lines of Divisional Posts. Remaining Coys. in Brigade Reserve in BELLACOURT.	

Mayer.
COMDG. 2nd ROYAL SCOTS FUSILIERS

SECRET.   VOLUME 3.

WAR DIARY

FOR THE MONTH OF DECEMBER 1916.

2ND BN ROYAL SCOTS FUSILIERS.

                                    R.G. Wallace
                                         Lieut. Colonel,
5-1-17.   Commanding 2nd Bn Royal Scots Fusiliers.

WAR DIARY or INTELLIGENCE SUMMARY

Army Form C. 2118.

Place	Date	Hour	Summary of Events and Information	Remarks and references to Appendices
SELLAROURT	1.12.16	—	Whole Bde Coys employed on R.E. Working parties & carrying for Special Coy. R.E.	S/C.E. 1/20,000
—	2.12.16	—	" " " " " " " " " " " " " " " "	
—	3.12.16	—	" " " " " " " " " " " " " " " " " LIEUT and A/ADJT. M. CARR proceeded to base on CADRES for a rest during which he will act as an instructor. MAJOR W. L. CAMPBELL attached ACTING ADJUTANT.	
—	4.12.16		Whole three Coys employed on R.E. Working parties & training for Special Coy R.E.	
—	5.12.16		Batts employed in turn on R.E. working parties, taking baths, & being fitted with box respirators.	
—	6.12.16		2nd R.S. Fus. relieved 17/15 MANCHESTER REGT in Right Sub-Sector. Relief completed by 11-45AM. Enemy quiet all day except for intermittent shelling between 11 AM & 3-30 pm during which time 20 TM rum shells were fired, during the changt.	
Source Farm	7.12.16		LIEUT-COL. R. K. WALSH. D.S.O. returning from leave re-assumed command of Btt. Batty. Lieut D H KENNEDY awarded MILITARY CROSS. Q.M.S. STILKINS, SGT. CASPER. L.), L/SGT. A. CHILCOTT, CPL. M. GRAND, H/CPLS A. HENDERSON & J. MOFFATT (Since killed in action), PTES. J. COOK, W. ALEXANDER, A. JACKSON & G. SLATTERY (late prisoner of War) awarded MILITARY MEDALS. Enemy shelled our line about 9 AM. 2 O.R. wounded. Work carried on during early morning. Enemy supervising. Work on Yesterday. Enemy artillery putting between 250 & 300 shells down.	
—	8.12.16		Work on Yesterday. Enemy artillery showed greater activity putting between 250 & 300 shells down the Bay, our artillery retaliated.	
—	9.12.16		Work on Yesterday. A much quieter period. MAJOR. W. L. CAMPBELL took command of "A" Coy. LIEUT J W WRIGHT acting on A/ADJT.	
—	10.12.16		Another quiet day although enemy artillery showed slightly greater activity than yesterday. T.M.R. as usual, mostly at night.	
—	11.12.16		Series activity on both sides. Our 10" H.T fired 10 rounds at enemy's line between 3 & 4 pm. No M.R as usual carried on.	
—	12.12.16		16&17th MANCHESTER REGT relieved the 2nd R.S. Fus. in the Right Subsector commencing at 9-30 AM. Relief completed by 12 noon. Batt. proceeded to Divisional reserve, Batt. HdQrs, Lewis Gunners, & D Coys billeted in BAILLEULVAL "A"& "B" Coys at BASSEUX. A/s pleased than positions in case of hostile shelling in 2 Hanover.	
BAILLEULVAL + BASSEUX	13.12.16		Batt. rested & cleaned up.	
—	14.12.16		Coy parades in morning. Coy. Offrs Air instruction in afternoon. Between 4-15 & 4-45pm enemy shelled Pillbox in BAILLEULVAL. A Coy rapidly proceeded to lettered bombardment positions. Several times hits were made on barracks hut but badly damaged gas alarm on 5-15 pm.	

WAR DIARY
or
INTELLIGENCE SUMMARY

(Erase heading not required.)

Army Form C. 2118.

Instructions regarding War Diaries and Intelligence Summaries are contained in F. S. Regs., Part II. and the Staff Manual respectively. Title Pages will be prepared in manuscript.

Place	Date	Hour	Summary of Events and Information	Remarks and references to Appendices
BAILLEUVAL + BASSEUX.	15.12.16.		Parades under Company arrangements. A working party of 120 OR under 2 Officers worked on cable trench in BRETTENCOURT. The C.O. 2nd in Command & 6 other officers made a reconnaissance of Duisans & Cojeul river lines in this area.	S/C.S.E. /24000
"	16.12.16		Working party for BRETTENCOURT as yesterday. Company & Battn. Parade. All available officers attended a demonstration w/ R/fle Grenade Spotters at Divisional Grenade School.	
"	17.12.16		Church Parade & Battn. Parade.	
TRENCHES	18.12.16		2nd R.S. 7us relieved the 11th MANR REGT. in the right Sub-Sector relief completed by noon. Brown.	
"	19.12.16		Quiet during relief, but showed a good activity during the afternoon. GAS ALERT on 10 A.M. A quiet day. Brown Stood on Support Line with 51st Stokes but were greatly silenced by our artillery. Work on trenches under RE & Company Supervision. Owing to the wet weather a portion of the front line had become impracticable. It was decided to evacuate the strongly wired F.P. Sap Line were taken in progress.	
"	20.12.16		Another quiet day. The Cheever atmosphere made it possible for service actions this were taken in Direction.	
"	21.12.16		Another quiet day. Work as usual by both sides. Wire & as usual. Hostile Artillery showed greater activity. Some 80 shells (77mm thg) being fired into the sub-section abreast of By both sides. French 100R as usual.	
"	22.12.16		During the day. Our artillery successfully replied. Brown Quieter. A patrol estimated at 15 strong approached a part of work on the wire in front of the trenches held by our Left front Coy. They dropped a bomb (presumably accidentally) & were seen by the aid of a very light, to make quickly back to their own line. The covering party to Brown Guns opened fire till its strength caused was inflicted. A patrol went out immediately but could find no trace of the hostile patrol. GAS ALERT off 5.30 pm	
"	23.12.16		Continuous rain made observation difficult & greatly hindered new work being carried on. All available men from Support Line Pact up to front Line to work the Pumps & assist in clearing the Pills in the trenches.	
"	24.12.16		We/A.S.H. were relieved by the 18th MANR REGT. Relief completed by 1 pm. Bn went into Brigade Reserve. HdQrs, A, B, & D Coys going w/ Bulk in BELLACOURT, the Coy holding the Posts in the Duisans Line. Bristol were afterled in the afternoon about 25 (77mm thg) were fired. GAS ALERT on 11 pm.	

Army Form C. 2118.

WAR DIARY
or
INTELLIGENCE SUMMARY
(Erase heading not required.)

Instructions regarding War Diaries and Intelligence Summaries are contained in F. S. Regs., Part II. and the Staff Manual respectively. Title Pages will be prepared in manuscript.

Place	Date	Hour	Summary of Events and Information	Remarks and references to Appendices
BELLACOURT	25/10/16		Xmas Day. Slakers trades.	51. C.S.E / 30000
"	26/10/16		A & B Coys on R.E. fatigue. Holders, +D Coy bathing Parade.	
"	27/10/16		D Coy Lewis gunners on RE fatigue, A+B Coys bathing Parade.	
"	28/10/16		B Coy, Scouts & Snipers on RE fatigue. D Coy relieving "C" Coy in the forests for 5 hours. "C" Coy bathing Parade.	
	29/4/16		B Coy + T.S.O.R. from A+D Coys on R.E. fatigue, remainder of A+D Coys, gun teams, fitting + Rifle inspection.	
Trenches	30/10/16		Bn relieved the 17 Bn Manchester Regt in the Right Sub-Sector. Disposition of Bn :- A.C.+D. Coys in the front line. B Coy - Reserve. Relief commenced at 10:30 am but owing to breaks of our communication trench were available after the strafe relief, was slowly made by & completed at 7.45 pm. Intermittent Artillery by both sides. Patrols turn patrols out during the night. One amoniam man put on strain, clearing trenches repairing the state of the trenches last under R.E. + company Supervision.	
"	31/10/16			

R L Webele
LIEUT: COLONEL
COMDG. 2nd ROYAL SCOTS FUSILIERS

VOLUME 3.

SECRET.

WAR DIARY.

FOR THE MONTH OF JANUARY, 1917.

2nd Bn. Royal Scots Fusiliers.

4.2.17.

[signature]
Major.
Commanding 2nd Bn. Royal Scots Fusiliers.

Army Form C. 2118.

Secret

WAR DIARY
or
INTELLIGENCE SUMMARY.
(Erase heading not required.)

Instructions regarding War Diaries and Intelligence Summaries are contained in F. S. Regs. Part II. and the Staff Manual respectively. Title pages will be prepared in manuscript.

Place	Date	Hour	Summary of Events and Information	Remarks and references to Appendices
TRENCHES	1.1.17		Hostile artillery not as active as usual. Work on trenches as before.	S/C S.E. 1/20000
"	2.1.17		Another quiet period. Work continued on trenches under Company R.E. supervision.	
"	3.1.17		Bn relieved by 1st/7th Bn Manchester Regt. Relief commenced 8.30 A.M. was completed at 12.15 p.m. Bn. HQ 9m, A,C & D Coy proceeded into billets in BELLACOURT, 'B' Coy occupying posts in Divisional line. A & D Coys found parties in afternoon for Battn Porters. Work carried on in the Posts in Divisional Line	
BELLACOURT	4.1.17		Bathing Parades. Enemy Artillery were active on the BASSEUX— BELLACOURT road, which they shelled with 5.9" How. from about 9 A.M — 1 P.M. Work carried on as usual in Divisional line	
BELLACOURT	5.1.17			
BELLACOURT	6.1.17		Work carried on as usual by the garrisons of the Posts in Divisional line	HONOURS — AWARDS: LIEUT. M. CARR M.C., No 18758 Sgt CHILCOTT No 10890 C.Q.M.S. WILKINS No 15146 Sgt McCARG No 8386 C.S.M. WOODWARD D.C.M. ...
BELLACOURT to HUMBERCOURT	7.1.17		The Bn march to billets in HUMBERCOURT. 'B' Coy the Bn from BELLACOURT and arrived at HUMBERCOURT at 3.30 p.m. 'B' Coy had been holding the posts in Divisional line, and was relieved by the 5th Bn. York and Lancaster Regiment at 8.30 p.m. In consequence 'B' Coy did not pass their starting point at BELLACOURT till 5.50 p.m. and they arrived at HUMBERCOURT at 10.45 p.m	
HUMBERCOURT	8.1.17		Bn rested & cleaned up	
"	9.1.17		C.O. went S/Cof route March.	
"	10.1.17		Musketry instruction. Following Officers joined from 4th Bn. 2nd Lieuts. W.L. INGLIS, A.D. LENNOX, E.A. SINCLAIR, W. TEMPLETON.	
"	11.1.17		Range Practice & Platoon training	

WAR DIARY
or
INTELLIGENCE SUMMARY.

Army Form C. 2118.

Place	Date	Hour	Summary of Events and Information	Remarks and references to Appendices
HUMBERCOURT	12.1.17	—	Platoon training	51 C 1/40,000
"	13.1.17	—	do. 2nd Lieut. Dougall joined the Bn.	
"	14.1.17	—	Church parade. Presentation of Medal Ribbons by G.O.C.	
"	15.1.17	—	G.O.C. 90th Brigade watched the Bn. by Capt. 20 Officers v 50 men employed on hut construction inspection at SUS-ST-LEGER at 11.A.M.	
"	16.1.17	—	Range Practices. Platoon Training. Battn. for A & B Coys.	
"	17.1.17	—	Heavy fall of snow during the night. Consequently all training was discontinued and men were employed in clearing roads.	
"	18.1.17	—	Training carried on as per Brigade Programme	
"	19.1.17	—	Inspection by G.O.C. of Bn. in progress of training	
"	20.1.17	—	Lieut. Colonel Watson D.S.O. proceeded to take over command of 6th Infantry Brigade	
"	21.1.17	—	Brigade Route March to SUS. ST. LEGER via LUCHEUX Forest. Church Parades. Major Campbell takes over command of Bn. Range Practices.	
"	22.1.17	—	Fresh Training starts as per Brigade Programme. Bayonet Fighting Course starts for officers & N.C.Os. P.T. and Bayonet Training. 2nd Lieutenant S. Fleming joins the Bn. Posted	
"	23.1.17	—	Range Practices. Bn. Training. 2nd Lieutenant S. Fleming joins the Bn. Posted to C Coy	
"	24.1.17	—	Bn. Training. Bayonet Fighting course. Rehearsal of Scheme with contact Aeroplanes. Lt. Col. Macnaghten D.S.O. takes command of Bn.	
"	25.1.17	—	Training & Range Practices as usual. 2nd Lieutenant A.C. McMaster joins the Bn.	
"	26.1.17	—	Bn. parades for Scheme with contact Aeroplanes. Specialists and Classes of instruction as usual	
"	27.1.17	—	Bn. Training. 150 men of A Coy & B Coy parade for wood-cutting fatigue at WATRON WOOD	
"	28.1.17	—	Church Parades. 150 men of C & D Coy parade for R.E. fatigue at WATRON WOOD. Inspection of Transport by Commanding Officer at 11 a.m. Kit Inspection by Coy Officers.	

Army Form C. 2118.

WAR DIARY
or
INTELLIGENCE SUMMARY.
(Erase heading not required.)

Instructions regarding War Diaries and Intelligence Summaries are contained in F. S. Regs., Part II. and the Staff Manual respectively. Title pages will be prepared in manuscript.

Place	Date	Hour	Summary of Events and Information	Remarks and references to Appendices
HUMBERCAMP	24.1.17		Inspection of Battn in progress of training by G.O.C. Carried out by platoons of B Coy. Classes of instruction and ranges as usual	LENS SHEET, 11
— " —	30.1.17		Training as usual. Then Coy. H.Q. Transport headed at 4 P.M. & marched via AUCHY EUX BOIS GROUCHY - DOULLENS & billets at AUTHIEULE arriving at 7.30 P.M.	
AUTHIEULE	31.1.17		Coy trades	
— " —			Battn entrained at R.E. Camp Sdg 2.30 P.M. & entrained from 12.45 P.M. till 4.30 P.M. Railway & Arrive STATION 7.30 P.M. Buttn 2nd NORTHUMBERLAND REAR Nguyen from F.A. P.U.	

Lt. Colonel
2nd ROYAL DUBLIN FUSILIERS.

Volumn 3.

S E C R E T.

W A R   D I A R Y

FOR THE MONTH OF FEBRUARY, 1917.

2nd BN. ROYAL SCOTS FUSILIERS.

IN THE FIELD.
28.2.17.

[signature] Major.
Commanding 2nd Bn. Royal Scots Fusiliers.

WAR DIARY or INTELLIGENCE SUMMARY

Army Form C. 2118.

Place	Date	Hour	Summary of Events and Information	Remarks and references to Appendices
AUTHIEULE	1-2-17		300 men employed on railway at AUTHIEULE STATION from 9 AM to 3.30 PM. 200 men employed in unloading material from 12.45 PM to 4 PM.	LENS SHEET
"	2-2-17		Working parties as above	
"	3-2-17		do. Bn HQ. & all surplus officers & men – over a detachment of 14 officers & 520 OR. Q.M. Stores & Transport marched to MONDICOURT via AMPLIER – HALLOY – GRENAS arriving at 3.30 PM	
MONDICOURT	4-2-17		Bn found and RE working party of 120 O.R. Cmd working parties found by detachment	
"	5-2-17		Working parties as above 2LT M W KENNEDY wound & 2LT LEISHMAN joined for duty	
"	6-2-17		do. Training & Specialist instruction	
"	7-2-17		do. do.	
"	8-2-17		do. do.	
"	9-2-17		Bn found additional RE working party of 150 OR causing all training to cease	
"	10-2-17		Working parties as usual	
"	11-2-17		do. do.	
"	12-2-17		do. do.	
"	13-2-17		do. do.	
"	14-2-17		do. do.	
"	15-2-17		do. do.	
"	16-2-17		do. do.	
"	17-2-17		do. do.	
"	18-2-17		Working parties as usual, except that during afternoon a party of 3 officers and 150 other ranks were employed unloading an ammunition train at MONDICOURT STN. LT COL M.E. M°CONAGHEY assumed over got Snr Bde the BRIG GEN LLOYD (on leave). MAJ. W.L. CAMPBELL assumed command of the Bn. LT M. CARR M.C. joined got out B.W.H.Q. G leave. CAPT R.A.Q. TAYLOR took on duties as Adjutant of the Bn. 2ND LT M.W. SMITH joined for duty. A draft of S.O.R. joined for duty.	
"	19-2-17		Number of Working Parties as usual. Work was carried on in a bog cutting about 2 kilometres up the line towards SAULTY.	

Army Form C. 2118.

WAR DIARY
or
INTELLIGENCE SUMMARY
(Erase heading not required.)

Instructions regarding War Diaries and Intelligence Summaries are contained in F. S. Regs., Part II. and the Staff Manual respectively. Title Pages will be prepared in manuscript.

Place	Date	Hour	Summary of Events and Information	Remarks and references to Appendices
MONDICOURT	20-2-17		Working Parties as usual. Heavy rain all day, making the earth very difficult to shovel.	
"	21-2-17		Working Parties as usual.	
"	22-2-17		Working Parties as usual.	
"	23-2-17		An extra working party of 100 men were found to work at Kilo. 48 under 110th Coy. R.E. This party was difficult to find, and Transport, Orderlies, servants etc. all had to be turned out. The extra party of 100 men again found. Other Working Parties as usual.	
"	24-2-17		" " " " " The large party of 250 broke off at 2.30 P.M. & returned to dinner. Draft of S.O.R. joined for duty.	
"	25-2-17		Both Working Parties again found.	
"	26-2-17		Extra Party of 100 no longer required. Party of 250 found as usual.	
"	27-2-17		Work as usual.	
"	28-2-17			

J Headrick Major
2nd ROYAL SCOTS FUSILIERS

Volume 3.

SECRET.

WAR DIARY

FOR THE MONTH OF MARCH, 1917.

2nd BN. ROYAL SCOTS FUSILIERS.

IN THE FIELD.
1.4.17.

Lieut.-Colonel.
Commanding 2nd Bn. Royal Scots Fusiliers.

WAR DIARY
or
INTELLIGENCE SUMMARY

(Erase heading not required.)

Army Form C. 2118.

Place	Date	Hour	Summary of Events and Information	Remarks and references to Appendices
MONDICOURT	1-3-17		Working Parties as usual.	
"	2-3-17		Working Parties as usual.	
"	3-3-17		Working Parties as usual.	
"	4-3-17		Working Parties as usual. Work stopped at 12.30 P.M.	
"	5-3-17		Working Parties as usual.	
"	6-3-17		Working Parties as usual.	
"	7-3-17		Working Parties as usual.	
"	8-3-17		Working Parties as usual. 1 Officer & 75 O.R. were working at WARLINCOURT STN	
"	9-3-17		Working Parties as usual. Same Party required at WARLINCOURT STN	
"	10-3-17		Working Parties as usual " "	
"	11-3-17		Working Parties at MONDICOURT ceased today. There was a parade as strong as possible for C.O.'s inspection followed by an hour's handling arms and steadying drill. Turn-out good. Working Party of 270 men found for digging a Picture ground, south of GRENAS & HALLOY. Work ceased at 2.0 P.M.	
"	12-3-17		Same Working Party found as yesterday. Work ceased at 12.30 P.M. on account of heavy rain. Party of 250 found for same work. Same Party found again	
"	13-3-17		Parade 9. A.M. Platoon training during morning. Draft of 6 O.R. joined for duty.	
"	14-3-17		All officers & men from Bn H.Q. and as many officers & N.C.O's as could be spared from Detachment together with representatives from all other Bns of the Bde assembled on the Picture Ground near GRENAS at 9.30 A.M. The ground were pointed out and explained by BRIG. GEN. LLOYD, after which the parade broke up into small parties and walked over it. Detachment joined Bn H.Q. at 10.0 P.M.	
"	15-3-17			
"	16-3-17			
"	17-3-17			

WAR DIARY
INTELLIGENCE SUMMARY

(Erase heading not required.)

Army Form C. 2118.

Place	Date	Hour	Summary of Events and Information	Remarks and references to Appendices
In the Field	18-3-17		Church Parade 9.30 A.M. No other work for the rest of the day. Received orders to move early on 19-3-17. Orders cancelled at 6.0 P.M.	
— " —	19-3-17		Bn relieved 2nd WILTS in BERNEVILLE – Parade 10.0 A.M. Brigade marched via LABRET – BAC DU SUD – BEAUMETZ – BERNEVILLE (Ref. map LENS–sheet 11) 2nd R.S.F. leading. Weather dry during march. Arrived in billets 4.0 P.M. Heavy rain soon after arrival. Owing to enemy with-drawal, the march up the ARRAS ROAD was countermanded.	
— " —	20-3-17		Orders received from Bde at 3.0 A.M. to move to OLD BRITISH LINE. S. of AGNY. Bn marched off at 1.0 P.M. Route followed – BERNEVILLE – BAC DU NORD – WAILLY – AGNY. Relieved 19TH MANCHESTERS in O.B.L. at 3.30 P.M. No shelling. Enemy has since retired beyond MERCATEL, but is still reported to be holding NEUVILLE VITASSE & TELEGRAPH HILL. Bn in dug-outs, so a large number of men had to construct bivouacs outside the whole Bn. MAJ. W.L. CAMPBELL proceeded to PONNIERA to take over command of 1st & K.L.R.	
— " —	21-3-17		Ref. Sheet 51.B.S.W. Right Half Bn on CARRYING work up to trenches near CHAT MAIGRE (A.G.(1) at M.27. a.3.4) in support. Nothing eventful during the day. A party of 4 officers & 4 N.C.O.s & 32 men per Coy proceeded to WAILLY for a "Decon Cay".	
— " —	22-3-17		Ref. Sheet 51.B.S.W. Right Half Bn marched up to old GERMAN trenchs near CHAT MAIGRE (H.Q. at M.27.a.3.4) in support to front line Bns. A large quantity of material was carried up to shelter constructors. The trenches have been fouled by the enemy and all the dug-outs blown in.	
— " —	23-3-17		Left half Bn moved up to join Rt half in MADELAINE REDOUBT commencing 9.30 A.M.	

WAR DIARY or INTELLIGENCE SUMMARY

Army Form C. 2118.

Place	Date	Hour	Summary of Events and Information	Remarks and references to Appendices
In the Field	24-3-17		Move successfully carried out by H.Q. arrived at 12.30 P.M. 17th MANCHESTERS in line that night. Orders received to relieve Relief commenced 12.0 Midnight & was reported complete at 2.45 A.M. 'A' Coy were left in shelter at CHAT MAIGRE. B'n was disposed as follows :- C & D Coys in front line, 2 Plats. 'B' Coy in Support, × 2 Platt in Reserve, with 16 of Bn MANCHR on right & 18th on left. Front line :- MARQUISE redoubt & line of BEAURAINS - MERCATEL Rd running through M.36.C. × M.36.a × C. SUPPORT LINE :- Sunken Rd running S. from MERCATEL through M.35.b. × a. Sunken Rd running through M.35.a × b. Reserve line — Morning quiet. In the afternoon all lines shelled with 4.2's & 77 m.m. Enemy didn't seem to know exactly where our lines lay. No Casualties.	
"	25-3-17		Shelling intermittent all through night. No damage. C.T. dug from front line to Support line (about 600 yds.) Wire put out. Line extended towards flanks but not completed. Day quiet. Patrols encountered no enemy.	
"	26-3-17		Intermittent shelling during night. No casualties. Mats were put out & C.T. continued. Day very quiet. G.we shelling continued as soon as night fell. Patrols encountered no enemy. 2nd LT MAYES admitted Fd Amb.	
"	27-3-17		Day quiet again. C.T. continued from Support line to Reserve line. Weather has cleared. Very few German e.T's.	
"	28-3-17		Relieved by 2nd WILTS, 21st Bde commencing 7.30 P.M. Night much quieter than usual & exceedingly dark. Relief took a long time. Platoons marched back independently. 'B' Coy to BLAIRVILLE QUARRIES with Bn H.Q. C & D. to FICHEUX. A Coy Rnd proceeded to BRETTENCOURT the night before.	

WAR DIARY
INTELLIGENCE SUMMARY
(Erase heading not required.)

Army Form C. 2118.

Place	Date	Hour	Summary of Events and Information	Remarks and references to Appendices
In the Field	28-3-17		Bullets fired. Most of the men were in old GERMAN dug-outs & same in bivouac	
" "	29-3-17		Day spent clearing up site. Continuous rain and thick mud. Bn. found 7 parties of 1 officer, N.C.O. & 30 men to construct a & new C.T. These parties moved off from CRUCIFIX – FICHEUX at 7.45 P.M. Draft of 7 O.R. joined for duty, including 2 Sergeants. Also 3 officers & 41 O.R. returned from Div. Depot. Officers – 2nd Lt J.V. SMITH, 2nd LT T. LEISHMAN, 2nd LT W. TEMPLETON.	
" "	30-3-17		Weather bad. Same parties found again for same work. A & B Coys had baths & clean change.	
" "	31-3-17		Same nothing parties found again. Draft of 12 Signallers joined for duty. Working party of 60 O.R. and 2 officers to continue work on C.T. under 201SE Coy. R.E.	

Volume 3.

SECRET.

WAR DIARY,

FOR THE MONTH OF APRIL, 1917.

2nd Bn. ROYAL SCOTS FUSILIERS.

IN THE FIELD.
30.4.17.

                                      Major.
Commanding 2nd Bn. Royal Scots Fusiliers.

Army Form C. 2118.

WAR DIARY
or
INTELLIGENCE SUMMARY
(Erase heading not required.)

Instructions regarding War Diaries and Intelligence Summaries are contained in F. S. Regs., Part II. and the Staff Manual respectively. Title Pages will be prepared in manuscript.

Place	Date	Hour	Summary of Events and Information	Remarks and references to Appendices
In the Field	1-4-17		Preliminary Operation Orders received from Bde. for Relief of 21st Bn Bde tomorrow. Also an order to the prepared to support the 21st Bde any time after Midnight 1st/2nd. Same working party of 600 found.	
"	2-4-17	8.30 AM	Digging Party of 4 Officers & 200 O.R. Orders received for two Coys. to move up to NAGPUR TRENCH in support of 21st Bde in HENIN. Party had just moved off when other order cancelled by 21st Bde, HENIN being reported taken.	
		8.15 P.M.	Bn. moved up to MADELAINE REDOUBT with orders to take over from centre Bn. of 21st B de an following night.	
"	3-4-17	11.0 AM.	Ordered to take over 1000 x of front of Rt Bn in addition to whole front of centre Bn. This gave us a front of some 2000 x extending from in front of MERCATEL to N. edge of HENIN.	
		8.0 P.M.	Relief commenced. A & C.Coy. moving into front line (C.Coy on Rt.), D.Coy in support, B.Coy. in Reserve. Details left behind at Transport lines were ordered up to Sunka Road near Bn. HQ as an extra reserve. Relief rendered much more difficult by the fact that we had to relieve 2 Bns., the front line consisting merely of a line of outpost in each case rather than sisting merely of a line of outposts.	
		2.30 AM	Relief reported complete.	
"	4-4-17		Weather very bad – cold & snowy. Main line of defence along a sunken road running parallel to the ARRAS–BAPAUME Rd & about 300 x in front of it. Outposts anything from 200 x to 500 x in front of Main Line of defence.	

WAR DIARY
or
INTELLIGENCE SUMMARY

Army Form C. 2118.

Place	Date	Hour	Summary of Events and Information	Remarks and references to Appendices
			The guns had moved up to their Battle Positions. A very large number of guns — chiefly 18 Pdrs & 4.5 Hows were situated in the COJEUL RIVER valley.	
		2.0 P.M.	Bombardment of enemy lines commenced.	
		8.0 P.M.	On account of our front being so extensive, 17th MANCH. REGT. relieved 'A' Coy in left sector of front thus leaving us some 1500 x. The other Coys. conformed to this move. During the night, 'C' Coy advanced its outposts from 200x - 300x. Small strong posts were constructed. These were occupied before dawn.	
5.4.17.			Our guns of all calibres bombarded the enemy lines all day, drawing no retaliation. Patrol:- In cooperation with Field guns & Howitzers a party of 16th MANCH. REGT. established their posts on the NEUVILLE-VITASSE — HENIN ROAD and found the village of HENIN at N.33.d.2.0 — N.32.b.7.7. & N.32.a.5.5., a strong post of 3 officers & 34 O.R. left as guard & made their way to an assembly Position 300 x W. of MŒUL at N.25.d.7.0. At 10.0 P.M. 12 Pdrs fired 6 salvos at MŒUL and Salvo being fired at 10.5 P.M. At that moment the mill was rushed from 3 sides & occupied. 1 Dying German was found & two escaped. The dead man was identified as a soldier of the 31st R.I.R. 1st Bn. 2nd Coy. Patrol then attempted to push forward to the road beyond the mill but it was held up by rifle & M.G. fire. Parties of enemy were endeavouring to surround its mill so the officer in charge decided to withdraw. Casualties (Wounded)	Ref. Map. S.B.S.W.

WAR DIARY or INTELLIGENCE SUMMARY

Army Form C. 2118.

(Erase heading not required.)

Place	Date	Hour	Summary of Events and Information	Remarks and references to Appendices
		11·0 P.M.	Another patrol of 1 Off & 4 O.R. attempted to reach the HINDENBURG LINE in order to examine the wire between N.26.c.2.9 & N.27.a.3.5. Three officers were made to get through but each time party was held up by enemy fire from its road. Returned after being out two hrs. Enemy artillery much more active. Both our lines & our guns received attention. Patrol. Another patrol was carried out on the same lines as last night. Strength 3 Off & 50 O.R. Party assembled near the Mill. From there they raided the wire & advanced towards sunken road. Three M.G's. were directed at them so party later about 70 x shalt of wood & remained there until 11·0 P.M. Meanwhile two parties each of 1 Off & 30 O.R. were constructing two advanced strong points. When raiding party returned, it left carrying parties to the strong points, which were completed by dawn and occupied. Another small party went to keep a Lewis gun team who put out between the two camp enemy's beyond dawn. Casualties during night :— 1 Killed, 4 missing 3 wounded	
	7-4-17		Quiet day. Front line shelled in the evening : 1 man killed in the evening: 1 man killed & 2 wounded	

WAR DIARY
INTELLIGENCE SUMMARY

Army Form C. 2118.

Place	Date	Hour	Summary of Events and Information	Remarks and references to Appendices
	7-4-17		Relieved by 2ND WILTS & 2ND BEDS. On Relief, Bn. marched back to assembly trenches at FICHEUX.	
	8-4-17	4.0 A.M.	Bn. had arrived & settled down in Bivouac. Fine sunny day.	
		3.0 P.M.	C.O's conference with Brigadier.	
	9-4-17		Z day.	
		12.0 N	Orders to be prepared to move at very short notice.	
		2.0 P.M.	Marched off in Fighting Order, coys marching at 300 x interval. Transport with Lewis S.A.A. flares etc. & Pack Mules with water accompanied Bn. Took up position in SWITCH LANE, S. of NEUCATEL. Officers & N.C.O's went on ahead to reconnoitre the country & positions of Bn. in the line. News that VIMY RIDGE & TELEGRAPH HILL were captured with 5000 prisoners & some guns.	
		8.30 P.M.	Hurried orders to move at once to take up a position in SUNKEN ROAD (near Support Line). Move completed by 12.0 M.N.	
	10-4-17	2.0 A.M.	Warning order to be prepared to support 8 & 9TH Bns in attack on HINDENBURG LINE	
		11.30 A.M.	Warning order to be prepared to side-step to the other side of NAGPUR TRENCH	
		4.0 P.M.	Above two orders cancelled, & orders received to make men as comfortable as possible. Soup, Rum & Tea issued. Night very cold. High wind & snow showers. Near that whole of MONCHY-LE-PREUX had fallen & cavalry were pushing on.	

WAR DIARY
or
INTELLIGENCE SUMMARY

Army Form C. 2118.

Place	Date	Hour	Summary of Events and Information	Remarks and references to Appendices
	10-4-17		Counter attack by enemy during night, a little ground regained S. of RIVER COTEUL.	
	11-4-17	11.0 AM	Orders to be prepared to move forward at 1.0 P.M. to support 16TH MARCH. Idea was to get through the wire of the HINDENBURG LINE where NAGPUR TRENCH joins it, using 'D' Coy as an advanced guard. 'D' Coy was then to form a flank guard to the other Coys coming up on the Right to free Batt to advance onto the Green Line E. of HENINEL.	
		12.30 P.M.	Move postponed till 3.0 P.M.	
		3.0 P.M.	Move cancelled. Bn. to go into CORPS RESERVE. 13,000 prisoners & 100 guns are reported taken. By nightfall the Divisions had cleared the HINDENBURG SYSTEM right down to the COTEUL.	
	12-4-17		Relieved by 2ND A & S.H. at 3.0 P.M. Marched to Billets in BAILLEULMONT. Arrived in billets about 9.0 P.M.	
	13-4-17		Paraded 10.0 A.M. Marched to FONQUEVILLERS, near GOMMECOURT. Arrived to find the whole village in ruins & no billets.	
		5.0 P.M.	Marched on to SOUASTRE, where whole Bn. was billeted in huts. 10ff & 70 O.R.	
	14-4-17		General cleaning up. Guard for Coy Prisoners Cage required.	
	15-4-17		In billets. Church Parade.	
	16-4-17		In billets. Training by Platoons.	
	17-4-17		In billets. Training in vicinity of CHATEAU-DE-LA-HAIE.	

WAR DIARY
or
INTELLIGENCE SUMMARY

(Erase heading not required.)

Army Form C. 2118.

Place	Date	Hour	Summary of Events and Information	Remarks and references to Appendices
	18-4-17	7.0 AM	Orders from Bde to move at 11.30 A.M. to vicinity of NEUVILLE VITASSE. Route followed via BIENVILLERS – ADINFER – BOIRY ST RICTRUDE – CHAT. MAIGRE – MERCATEL – NEUVILLE-VITASSE. Total distance of 17 miles. There were two long halts for dinners at tears. Rain nearly all day. Arrived in HINDENBURG SYSTEM just E. of NEUVILLE-VITASSE at 9.0 P.M. without a single man having fallen out. Men made shelters & snooze in the trenches. Orders to relieve Front line.	
	19-4-17	3.0 P.M.	A & C Coys. moved off to go into support in Sunken Cross Roads and road running through N.23.d.	
		7.30 P.M.	H.Q. & B & D Coys. moved up. B & D Coys taking over front line. Casualties:- 1 Killed 8 wounded (O.R.)	
	20-4-17		Shelling during whole day. 2 O.R. wounded, 1 killed. Preliminary orders for attack.	
	21-4-17		Another day of continuous shelling on both sides. B⁴ H.Q. moved forward to S. side of RIVER COTEUL. Preliminary orders for attack given to O.C. Coys. Casualties:- 2 O.R. killed, 1 wounded, 2 shell-shock.	
	22-4-17		Conference of O.C. Coys. with C.O. Final arrangements for attack and Operation Orders sent out. 5 more casualties in "A" Coy.	

WAR DIARY or INTELLIGENCE SUMMARY

Army Form C. 2118.

Place	Date	Hour	Summary of Events and Information	Remarks and references to Appendices
	3.4.17	1.0 A.M.	Bn. in assembly positions by 1.0 A.M. Objective: - To advance to "BLUELINE" - the high ground overlooking CHERISY & the SENSEE Valley.	
		4.45 A.M.	Zero. Our guns opened an exceedingly heavy barrage, which was almost instantly replied to by nearly as heavy a one by the enemy on our front line & Supports. Bn advanced on a 2 Coy. front, 2 platoons of each Coy. in each of 4 waves. A & B Coys. Right, C & D at left. Even platoon went off exactly to time and kept its direction except for the right platoon which bore slightly too much to the right. The enemy instantly opened a heavy M.G. barrage which held up nearly the whole line. Those men that escaped pushed on most gallantly, but were eventually stopped long before reaching their objective. H.Q. followed at Zero + 20. Pushing that our line had advanced much further than it had, the Colonel & Adjutant pushed on. They were confronted by enemy M.G.s not 100 yds. away and forced into shell holes, the Colonel being killed.	
		6.0 A.M.	Enemy attempted a local counter-attack to roll up our right flank. He succeeded in reaching our position, but was then caught in one of our Lewis guns, and held up, leaving many dead.	

WAR DIARY or INTELLIGENCE SUMMARY

Army Form C. 2118.

Place	Date	Hour	Summary of Events and Information	Remarks and references to Appendices
In the Field	23.4.17	12.0 Noon	Message received from Bde. that enemy were strongly counter-attacking 150th Bde on left. H.Q.I. & what men were left stood-to in the front line, but the attack did not extend to our front.	
		6.0 P.M.	Enemy line was again heavily barraged, and the 21st Bde attacked, supported in exactly the same way as we had been in our attack in the morning. The enemy line on the left were occupied, but they were again held up on the right and were caught in an exceedingly heavy barrage which the enemy put down in retaliation. Orders received to get whole Bn. out of the line before attack at 6.0 P.M.	
		4.30 P.M.	By 9.0 P.M. all survivors of the battle were back in the Reserve position. Casualties Officers:- Killed in action:- Lt.Col. M.E. McCONAGHEY D.S.O. — 2Lt. T. SPEARS — 2LT. T. LEISHMAN — 2LT. H.F. SMITH — 2LT. J.C. CAMERON. Died of Wounds:- 2LT. J. McLEOD. Wounded in action:- 2LT. D.B. MACKENZIE — 2LT. F. ROBB — 2LT.V. SMITH — 2LT. A.C. McMASTER — 2LT. J.T. FRASER. Missing:- 2LT. E.A. SINCLAIR — 2LT. D. TRENCH. — 2LT. T.S. CAMPBELL. Wounded & Missing:- 2LT. G. DICEY. Casualties Other Ranks:- Killed in action 55. Wounded 195. Missing 209. Died of wounds 3.	

Army Form C. 2118.

WAR DIARY
or
INTELLIGENCE SUMMARY

(Erase heading not required.)

Instructions regarding War Diaries and Intelligence Summaries are contained in F. S. Regs., Part II. and the Staff Manual respectively. Title Pages will be prepared in manuscript.

Place	Date	Hour	Summary of Events and Information	Remarks and references to Appendices
In the Field	24-4-17		Marched back to NEUVILLE-VITASSE area. Roll-calls, casualty reports, etc.	
	25-4-17		The bodies of LT.COL. McCONAGHEY, D.S.O. & 2 LT. McLEOD were recovered. Bn. Bivouacs at NEUVILLE-VITASSE.	
	26-4-17		" " " Burial of LT. COL. McCONAGHEY. D.S.O. & 2 LT McLEOD MAJ. W.L. CAMPBELL rejoined & took over command.	
	27-4-17	11.0AM	Marched off to entrain at ARRAS for HERMICOURT, N. of ST. POL. Transport left AGNY at 2.0 P.M. to do road. Arrived ARRAS 4.0 P.M. Entrained 7.0 P.M. Left 9.0 P.M. Arrived ST. POL. about 2.0 A.M. Marched to HERMICOURT, arriving 4.30 A.M.	
	28-4-17		Cleaning up, Refitting etc. Church Parade. CAPT. J.B. ORR – 2 LT. J.R.D. SMITH – 2 LT. W. TEMPLETON – 2 LT. T.W. NELSON rejoined the Bn. for duty	
	29-4-17			
	30-4-17		Parades under Coy. Arrangements	

J. McNeile — Major
LIEUT. COLONEL,
COMDG. 2nd ROYAL SCOTS FUSILIERS.

Volume 3.

2ND BATTALION,
THE ROYAL SCOTS
FUSILIERS.

SECRET.

WAR DIARY

FOR THE MONTH OF MAY, 1917.

2nd BN. ROYAL SCOTS FUSILIERS.

IN THE FIELD.
4.6.17.

Lieut.-Colonel.
Commanding 2nd Bn. Royal Scots Fusiliers.

WAR DIARY
INTELLIGENCE SUMMARY

Army Form C. 2118.

Place	Date	Hour	Summary of Events and Information	Remarks and references to Appendices
In the Field	1-5-17		In Billets in HERNICOURT. Training under Company arrangements. Two drafts - 10 4/18 O.R & 10 14 O.R. joined for duty.	
"	2-5-17		Maj. Gen. J. de L. WILLIAMS C.M.G. D.S.O. assumed command of the Division vice Maj Gen T.S.M. SHEA C.B. D.S.O. The new Divisional Commander visited the Bn. In Billets in HERNICOURT. Warning that Bn will move by MT on 3-5-17 received at 1.20 PM.	
"	3-5-17		Moved off at 9.0 AM. Marched via PIERREMONT - BEAUVOIS - OEUF - WILLEMAN - WAIL to VACQUERIETTE. Dinners eaten near WILLEMAN. Arrived in Billets about 3.30 PM.	
"	4-5-17		In Billets. Training in Training Area. D.Coy on Range.	
"	5-5-17		A Coy & part of B Coy on Range. Rest of Battn in Training Area. Attack practise	
"	6-5-17		Church Parades. Baths. Sgts S.I. How joined for duty	
"	7-5-17		A Coy & remainder of B Coy on Range. Rest of Bn attack practise in Training Area.	
"	8-5-17		Parades cancelled because of rain. Kit inspections. Parade in afternoon. Drafts of 38 O.R. joined for duty.	
"	9-5-17		Usual Training in Training area & firing on Range.	
"	10-5-17		Brigade Operations in the morning. Draft of 4 officers & 170 O.R. joined for duty. Named Officers:- 2 Lt J.J. BROWN, 2 Lt R.N. DEWAR, 2 Lt F.A. ALLAN, 2 Lt I. RIDDEL	

Army Form C. 2118.

WAR DIARY
or
INTELLIGENCE SUMMARY
(Erase heading not required.)

Instructions regarding War Diaries and Intelligence Summaries are contained in F.S. Regs., Part II and the Staff Manual respectively. Title Pages will be prepared in manuscript.

Place	Date	Hour	Summary of Events and Information	Remarks and references to Appendices
In the Field	11.5.17	—	Training and Musketry. Competition between 1 Platoon of each unit of Bde.	LENS MAP SHEET 11
"	12.5.17	—	Supper to (Ceremonial) by Corps Commander.	HAZEBROUCK SHEET 5A.
"	13.5.17	—	Church Parade. Draft of 6.O.R. joined for duty.	
"	14.5.17	—	Training in Training Area. 'A' Coy carried out small Field Firing practice	
"	15.5.17	—	Training during morning. In the afternoon, Sports were held between 1st March. & anniversary.	
"	16.5.17	—	Training & Musketry. Heats run off to decide in Competitors for Div. Sports.	
"	17.5.17	—	Parade Cancelled on account of rain.	
VACQUERIETTE	18.5.17	—	Usual Training & Musketry Parades. Supp: to London Gazette dated 1.5.17 NºA7160	
" "	19.5.17	—	" " " SGT W. HOGG awarded "Medaille Militaire" (Extract PART II ORDERS No 28 dated 19.5.17)	
" "	20.5.17	—	Bn paraded at 9 A.M. and marched in Brigade Column via ERQUIÈRES-GALAMETZ-FILLIÈVRES-LINZEUX to HÉRICOURT arriving 2 P.M.	
HÉRICOURT	21.5.17	—	Bn paraded 9 A.M. and marched via CROISETTE - ST.POL - WAVRANS - HESTRUS to TANGRY arriving 3 P.M. Dinners en route.	
TANGRY	22.5.17	—	Bn paraded 9 A.M. and marched via FIEFS-FONTAINE AUCHY AU-BOIS to RELY arriving 2.30 P.M.	
RELY	23.5.17	—	Brigade rested.	
"	24.5.17	—	Bn paraded at 11.15 A.M. and marched to LAMBRES arriving 12.15 P.M.	

Army Form C. 2118.

WAR DIARY
or
INTELLIGENCE SUMMARY
(Erase heading not required.)

Place	Date	Hour	Summary of Events and Information	Remarks and references to Appendices
LAMBRES	25.5.17		Bn paraded at 7.45.A.M. and marched in rear of Brigade via PRADELLES- STEENBECQUE- MORBECQUE- HAZEBROUCK to LA KREULE arriving 4 P.M. dinner taken en route	HAZEBROUCK SHEET 5A.
LA KREULE	26.5.17	—	Coy parades	
—	27.5.17	—	Church parades	
—	28.5.17	—	Bn Outpost scheme practised.	
—	29.5.17	—	Coy parades.	
—	30.5.17	—	"Baltimores" by motor Bus to MORINGHEM arriving 12 midday	
LAKREULE	31.5.17			

[signature]

LIEUT: COLONEL,
COMDG. 2nd ROYAL SCOTS FUSILIERS.

Volume 3.

S E C R E T.

WAR DIARY

FOR THE MONTH OF JUNE, 1917.

2nd Bn. ROYAL SCOTS FUSILIERS.

IN THE FIELD.
2-7-17

[signature]
Lieut.-Colonel.
Commanding 2nd Bn. Royal Scots Fusiliers.

WAR DIARY or INTELLIGENCE SUMMARY

Army Form C. 2118.

Secret

Place	Date	Hour	Summary of Events and Information	Remarks and references to Appendices
MORINGHEM	1.6.17		Parades & inspections under Company arrangements	
	2.6.17		Bn. field implements for training and area allotted. D Coy. carried out rifle practices, in the afternoon, sheet in billy MORRISON	
	3.6.17		Church Parades. Both Presbyterians & Church of England Batt. for billy. Visit. Capt. W.E. MAIR sheet. A.S. TAYLOR joined	
	4.6.17		All companies carry out a field firing practice on the Range.	
	5.6.17		Corps Commander's parade from 9.30 a.m. till 12 noon. Training area & open formations under Coy arrangements in training area	
	6.6.17		Bn. marks by road to train to ARBRE about 1 mile W. of POPERINGHE. Bn. headed to starting point by 5.30 am & marches to ST OMER where they entrained by 8.30 am. Train arrived outside POPERINGHE by about 11.30 am. The outskirts of POPERINGHE were being shelled with "stream gun" at that time.	
ARBRE	7.6.17		March to billets close to ARBRE. Honours & Awards- No.1009. Cpl. T. IRONSIDE. D.C.M. under D.R.O. 6.6.17. Company held Kit inspections under their own arrangements. Capt. J.E UTTERSON-KELSO. 2Lt. P.D. MORRISON. 2Lt W.R. FLEMING 2Lt H.R. HOLME joined the Bn. for duty. MAJOR A. KING leaves the Bn. Sick.	
	8.6.17		Bn. warned to proceed to the trenches in the evening. Bn. rests during the day preparatory to marching in the evening. March to POPERINGHE STATION & entraining the train took us up the line as far as it was considered safe. From there we marched to outskirts of YPRES where we met our guides. Marched to trenches we relieved the 17th K.L.R in the support Bn. trenches. Relief complete about 2 am. Nil casualties during relief	

Army Form C. 2118.

WAR DIARY
INTELLIGENCE SUMMARY
(Erase heading not required.)

Instructions regarding War Diaries and Intelligence Summaries are contained in F.S. Regs., Part II. and the Staff Manual respectively. Title Pages will be prepared in manuscript.

Place	Date	Hour	Summary of Events and Information	Remarks and references to Appendices
In the field	9.6.17		Bn relieved in the support Bn line by the 1/7 MANCHESTER REGT and proceeded to take over the front line from the 1/9 K.L.R. Disposition as follows — 1 Company in the front line, also judging garrisons for the Hole in Reserve front, 2 Companies in the Support line, 1 Company in Reserve. The support line was the ELLIS LEINSTER STREET, MAYREAUVE line RITZ STREET. On Sector was the HOOGE Sector. Relief complete about 2 am.	
	10.6.17		The enemy artillery did not show great activity except against our batteries which he shelled intermittently. He used a great number of gas-shells both lachrymatory & asphyxiating against our batteries during the early morning. Enemy artillery being quiet the day passed quietly. One of our planes marked activity on part of the enemy around 6.30 pm. During the bright dawn behind the enemy lines 1.8.6. 1 — 8 and 9.7. Two enemy M.Gs. spotted at 1.8.6. 1 — 8 and 9.7. (Ref. ZILLEBEKE 6" Trench map. SHEET 28. N.W.)	
	11.6.17		On the 11th/12th we sent out 2 officers patrols. They were fixed.	
	12.6.17		Enemy artillery quiet during the morning. From 2.30 p.m. till 6.40 about 1500 shells were distributed on LEINSTER STREET, OXFORD STREET and WEST STREET. Calibre of gun which fired was "5.9". How. Considerable damage was done but luckily the casualties were slight. He again shelled battery positions for about 4 or 5 hours with gas-shells. At 11 p.m. a mine was sprung by the enemy on our left. Brigade	

WAR DIARY or INTELLIGENCE SUMMARY

Army Form C. 2118.

Place	Date	Hour	Summary of Events and Information	Remarks and references to Appendices
In the Field	13.6.17		At 3 a.m. a mine was sprung. Another mine was sprung shortly afterwards. At 12.15 p.m. enemy artillery opened heavy bombardment on LEINSTER STREET trenches. At 3.30 a.m. another heavy bombardment on LEINSTER STREET trenches at the 1.30 p.m. At 2 p.m. he started again, at the Manchester 6 p.m. Most of these shells were 4.2". The rain was bad. Regiment raided the Enemy took prisoners. The under barrage fire from our field guns. At 10.30 p.m. we sent out a patrol of 1 officer + 6 O.R. in order to procure identification. The objective was the sap running down the S. side of the MENIN road about 150 yards from the CULVERT. The sap was heavily wired in a semi-circular form round the MENIN road & quite impassable. No prisoners were taken. The patrol returned along the MENIN road, arriving back about 12 midnight. (Ref. ZILLEBEKE Trench map. Sheet 28.S.W.) Enemy artillery again active on LEINSTER STREET. Receiving in some 10 yards of trench. The 1st Bn. WORCESTER REGIMENT relieved us that night, relief being completed about 2.45 a.m. the Bn. moved to CHATEAU SEGARD. During the march down, asphyxiating gas was encountered at heavy shell fire was met especially in the region of SHRAPNEL CORNER (by several casualties occurred. We arrived at our destination 5.30 a.m.	

WAR DIARY
of
INTELLIGENCE SUMMARY

(Erase heading not required.)

Army Form C. 2118.

Place	Date	Hour	Summary of Events and Information	Remarks and references to Appendices
In the Field	15-6-17		Bn in bivouacs near CHATEAU SEGARD. Two fatigue parties found at 8.15 P.M. & 8.45 P.M. of 160 all ranks to camp material from ZILLEBEKE DUMP. Draft of 11 O.R. joined for duty.	
	16-6-17		Bn in bivouacs. Some fatigue parties found. 2 O.R. wounded.	
	17-6-17		Bn in bivouacs. Some fatigue parties found. Draft of 6 O.R. joined for duty.	
	18-6-17		Bn moved to ENGLISH WOOD in order to relieve the garrison in CHATEAU SEGARD WOOD. One working party of 160 all ranks found. Recommended for Distinguished Conduct in the Field { No.10388 Pte NORRIS.A. No.90322 - BARRETT.	
	19-6-17		Bn in bivouacs in ENGLISH WOOD. Two fatigue parties found — one of 128 all ranks and one of 50. Two Coys. had to take shelter in dugouts during the night owing to shelling.	
	20-6-17	8.30 P.M.	Bn moved back to OTTOWA CAMP near OUTERDOM at 6.0 P.M. Settled in Camp. Draft of 8 O.R. joined for duty.	
	21-6-17	8.0 A.M. 3.15	Bn paraded and marched to RENINGELST station where it entrained. Entrained at WATTEN, 12 miles from ST OMER. Thence by march route to POLINCOVE, through FORÊT D'EPERLECQUES. Settled in billets by 6.30 P.M.	
	22-6-17		Parade 9.0 A.M. Bn proceeded by march route to TOURNEHEM via ZOUAFQUES (5 miles). Arrived in billets about 11.0 A.M.	
	23-6-17		Bn in billets in TOURNEHEM. Commanding Officer's inspection of Coys. in turn. Cleaning up etc.	
	24-6-17 25-6-17		Bn in billets in TOURNEHEM. Church parades.	
	26-6-17		Attack Practice in conjunction with 17th March. Regt. Battns. Preliminary Operation order received for move to OTTOWA CAMP. Final order received at 7.30 P.M.	
	27-6-17		Bn marched off at 6.30 A.M. and proceeded by WATTEN Stn. Entrained by 10.0 A.M. Arrived at ABEELE.	

Army Form C. 2118.

WAR DIARY
or
INTELLIGENCE SUMMARY
(Erase heading not required.)

Instructions regarding War Diaries and Intelligence Summaries are contained in F. S. Regs., Part II. and the Staff Manual respectively. Title Pages will be prepared in manuscript.

Place	Date	Hour	Summary of Events and Information	Remarks and references to Appendices
In the Field	27-6-17		at 1.30 P.M. Thence by march route to OTTOWA CAMP. Settled in camp by 4.30 P.M. One draft of 4 officers & 20 O.R. and another of 50 O.R. joined for duty. Capt. D.H. Kennedy rejoined the Bn. from II Corps School, and took over command of Letter "B" Coy.	
	28-6-17		Parade 9.30 A.M. Bn. moved to CANAL RESERVE CAMP, near DICKEBUSH. 3 Working Parties found, 2 of 100 all ranks and one of 2 Coys, the two first to work on the Light Railway near BEDFORD HOUSE under 7th Bn. C.R.T. and the second to dig a cable trench from ZILLEBEKE BUND.	
	29.6.17		"B" in CANAL RESERVE CAMP. WORKING PARTY furnished to work on Light Railway as before. 100 all ranks more than usual. Draft of 8 O.R. joined for duty.	
	29.6.17		Bn in CANAL RESERVE CAMP. Heavy rain all day. Two working parties of 50 all ranks each furnished for work on Light Railways.	

W. Henderson
LIEUT. COLONEL,
COMDG. 2nd ROYAL SCOTS FUSILIERS.
1-7-17.

2nd R. SCOTS FUSILIERS
ORDERLY ROOM.
Date 5-8-17
No. 0449

Volume 3.

32A.
è verso
90/30

SECRET.

WAR DIARY

FOR THE MONTH OF ~~MAY~~ July 1917.

2nd Bn. ROYAL SCOTS FUSILIERS.

IN THE FIELD.
~~4-8-17.~~
5·8·17

[signature]
Lieut.-Colonel.
Commanding 2nd Bn. Royal Scots Fusiliers.

Captain for

WAR DIARY or INTELLIGENCE SUMMARY

Army Form C. 2118.

Place	Date	Hour	Summary of Events and Information	Remarks and references to Appendices
In the Field	1-7-17		Church Parades. Working Party of 250 all Ranks for digging cable trench. Enemy for less active both with his artillery & in the air. Bn. won Stomp-Paul Trowel-Digging Competition (2 Platoons from each Bn. in the Bde.)	
"	2-7-17		Same working party of 2 Cys. Found Parties comprised part of the day in Motor Lorries. Weather fine - visibility very clear. Great aeroplane activity on both sides. Camp shelled intermittently all through the night.	
"	3-7-17		Same Working Party of 2 Coys. furnished for cable track construction.	
"	4-7-17		Camp shelled in the Early morning. One shell obtained a direct hit on the Transport Lines. Casualties :- 9 horses killed, 4 wounded; 3 O.R. killed & 5 wounded.	
"	5-7-17		Same working Party furnish for cable trench construction. Officers carried out reconnaissance of assembly trenches. Operation Orders received for move to Back Area on following day. Draft of 3 O.R. joined for duty.	
"	6-7-17		Bn. marched off from CANAL RESERVE CAMP at 6.45 A.M., halted for four hour in the vicinity of RENINGHELST, and entrained at RENINGHELST STN at 2.0 P.M. Transport moved by road. Bn. arrived at WATTEN at 6.30 P.M. detrained and marched to POLINCOVE through the FORET D'EPERLECQUES. Settled in billets by 10.0 P.M.	
"	7-7-17		Parade 10.30 A.M. Marched to LANDRETHUN-LES-ARDRES x YEUSE via ZUT-KERQUE & NIELLES-LES-ARDRES. Settled in billets by 2.30 P.M.	

WAR DIARY
or
INTELLIGENCE SUMMARY

(Erase heading not required.)

Army Form C. 2118.

Place	Date	Hour	Summary of Events and Information	Remarks and references to Appendices
In the Field	8-7-17		Church Parade. Cleaning up etc.	
"	9-7-17		Musketry etc. in Billets. 4 O.R (Signallers) joined for duty	
"	10-7-17		Musketry etc. in Billets	
"	11-7-17		Attack Practice on TOURNEHEM Picture Ground.	
"	12-7-17		Attack Practice on TOURNEHEM picture ground. O.R joined for duty	
"	13-7-17		Baths & lectures in Billets. Maj. T.C Whigham. M.C. joined for duty. Draft of 16	
"	14-7-17		Early morning attack on picture ground by whole Division. Back in billets by 7.30 A.M.	
"	15-7-17		Draft of 2 O.R joined for duty. Church Parades in the morning. Divisional Horse Show in the afternoon.	
"	16-7-17		Divisional attack practice over the Picture Ground. Transport paraded Bde starting point at 10.45 A.M. to march by road to the WIPPENHOEK AREA, stopping in the NOORDPEENE AREA for the night.	
"	17-7-17		Bn. entrained at 3.30 P.M. to move to the WIPPENHOEK AREA. The Bn Bus convoy was formed up with its head on WOLPHUS on the main CALAIS-ST OMER ROAD facing East. The convoy moved via ST OMER, S. of CASSEL, & STEENVORDE where there was a halt of 1 hour for teas. Arrived in PATRICIA CAMP, near WIPPENHOEK at about 12.0 Midnight.	
"	18-7-17		Rest & cleaning up. Some rain.	
"	19-7-17		Bn. in PATRICIA CAMP Parades under Coy arrangements. 2LT D B MACKENZIE joined for duty	
"	20-7-17		Bn. paraded at 5.30 A.M. & marched to Billets near STEENVORDE via ABEELE. Onwards	

WAR DIARY
or
INTELLIGENCE SUMMARY

(Erase heading not required.)

Army Form C. 2118.

Place	Date	Hour	Summary of Events and Information	Remarks and references to Appendices
In the Field	20-7-17		in billets about 8.30 A.M. Came under the orders of 89th Bde while in this area.	
"	21-7-17		Training under Coy. arrangements. Firing on the Range. Lecture to officers in afternoon.	
"	22-7-17		Church Parade. Draft of 18 O.R. joined Div. Reinforcement Camp, and were taken on the strength of the Bn.	
"	23-7-17		Training under Coy. arrangements. Regimental Sports in the afternoon.	
"	24-7-17		Bn. started at 6.15 A.M. and proceeded by march route to PATRICIA CAMP via STEENVOORDE & ABEELE, arriving camp about 10.0 A.M. Rest for the remainder of the day. Op. Order for move forward to CHATEAU SEGARD on 25-7-17 received. Op. Order postponed. Inspections etc. under Company arrangements.	
"	25-7-17		Bn. still in PATRICIA CAMP awaiting orders. Parades inclusive Route March in the morning and with Coy arrangements in the afternoon.	
"	26-7-17		Operation Order hopes move to CHATEAU SEGARD is put again. Bn. entrained at times elsewhere afternoon(?)hed. Patricia Camp awaiting news. Draft J/S OR arrived Bn. Stat at Patricia Camp. Bn. arrived at CHATEAU	
"	26-7-17		Op. order for move out into line again. 2 Coys & WELLINGTON CRES (Assist B.) SEGARD about 9 P.M.	
	27-7-17		Order received to move forward - 2 Cos & WELLINGTON CRES (Assist B) 1 Co. & ZILLEBEKE BUND, 1 Co and Bn. HQ. G BEDFORD HOUSE (Sh 28)R - move completed by 11.30 P.m.	

WAR DIARY or INTELLIGENCE SUMMARY

Army Form C. 2118.

Place	Date	Hour	Summary of Events and Information	Remarks and references to Appendices
30th June	30/7/17	3pm	Orders received that ZERO day would be 31/7/17. Bn. throw up no arranged trenches or arranged in A and B Coys and Bn. HQrs.	
			A Heavy Trench mortar barrage was laid down on WELLINGTON CRESCENT (MAPLE TRENCH — C and D Coys to throw up Bns.)	
	4 Sep		Orders received that ZERO hour to be at 3.50 am 31st. Coys to move from present positions straight to forward assembly positions in No Man's Land.	
		9.30pm	Head of WARRINGTON AVENUE. C Coy and Bn. HQrs. moved up to MAPLE TRENCH during the night. 12 midnight D Coy moved from BUN II & taught to forward assembly positions.	
	31/7/17	12.30 am	A and B Coys moved from WELLINGTON CRES. to forward positions, followed by C Coy and Bn. HQrs.	
		3.30 am	The Bn. was in No Man's Land' clear of our front line, waiting for ZERO. Disposition according to instructions to lt. J/ferrin operations issued to Bn. and also forwarded to Bri in record at TOURNEHEM.	

WAR DIARY
or
INTELLIGENCE SUMMARY
(Erase heading not required.)

Army Form C. 2118.

Place	Date	Hour	Summary of Events and Information	Remarks and references to Appendices
Spotsbulm	31/7/17	3:20am	The Bn moved to attack on a two Batt front. 16th and 18th MANCHESTERS to lead in front of STIRLING CASTLE - to CLAPHAM JUNCTION - and SURBITON VILLAS. The 2nd RSF and 17th MANCHESTERS to leapfrog through and attack "BLACKLINE" running in front of JHEROUTHAGE CHATEAU to the N. side of GLENCORSE WOOD II (ZILLEBEKE Trench Map E.II.S). BATN dropped in 4 waves: No 1 wave "A" Coy to Captain 2 Stray Point in front of BLACKLINE. No 2 wave "B" Coy to Captain Shell trench in front of BLACKLINE. No 3 wave "C" and "D" Coys to Cap line and beyond to BLACKLINE.	16th & 18th MANCHESTERS
	31/7/17	3:50	ZERO Coys advanced under Barrage. Enemy keep heavy indeed second behind barrage support a barrage Coys took up Sweep at their point of assembly & BLUE line and pushed on to jouty Gory offensive in front of BLUE line	
		6am		

WAR DIARY
or
INTELLIGENCE SUMMARY
(Erase heading not required.)

Army Form C. 2118.

Place	Date	Hour	Summary of Events and Information	Remarks and references to Appendices
	3/11/17	6.30A	Bns held up about 200 x in front of 'BLUE LINE'. Suffered casualties from M. Guns and rifle fire. 6 L's captured 2 M. Guns and 50 prisoners at Railway Embankment (S.E. of MENIN ROAD). 'B' Coy captured 23 prisoners in front of STIRLING CASTLE. 'A' & 'D' BLUE LINE. Coys held up in front of blockhouses.	
		8.0AM	The 89th Bde came up but were held up before they reached the BLUE LINE and dug in.	
		10.0AM	The 18th Div. arrived and came through the 30th Div. But they were unable to push forward and were held up about 200 x in front of our line.	
		2.0P.M	Enemy bombardment of near positions commenced. It continued until 6.0 P.M. with a stint break from about 3.15 P.M. till 4.0 P.M. Fairly severe casualties resulted, but the position was held. The enemy attempted a small counter attack, but it was immediately repulsed.	
		6.0PM	Word was passed down the line that all troops of 90th Bde were to withdraw. About half the garrison of the BLUE LINE did not	

got the message till much later, and consequently did not leave the line until early the next morning. The remainder of the Bn. went track to ZILLEBEKE PROMENADE.

WAR DIARY

of the 2nd Battalion, Royal Scots Fusiliers

for the month of August 1917.

VOLUME (3)

                                  Lt. Colonel

1.9.1917   Commanding 2nd Bn., Royal Scots Fusiliers

WAR DIARY or INTELLIGENCE SUMMARY

Army Form C. 2118.

Place	Date	Hour	Summary of Events and Information	Remarks and references to Appendices
In the Field	1-8-17		By 9:0 A.M. most of the Bn had returned to ZILLEBEKE PROMENADE. There had been heavy rain all night, & it continued to rain all day. Enemy shelled the BUND & PROMENADE with a heavy high velocity shell. 14 casualties resulted.	
		2.0 P.M.		
		3.0 P.M.	Orders received from Bde to return to CHATEAU SÉGARD area. Bn went back by small parties & bivouacked near CAFÉ BELGE. Heavy rain all day.	
	2-8-17		Bn in bivouacs in CHATEAU SÉGARD area. Orders received from Bde to move back to PATRICIA CAMP the following day. Heavy rain all day.	
	3-8-17		Bn entrained at 1.30 P.M. & arrived at PATRICIA CAMP about 3.30 P.M. in heavy rain. However, tents were pitched & the men made themselves comfortable.	
	4-8-17		Bn moved by train & march route to ST SYLVESTRE CAPPEL, arriving about 4.30 P.M. Still heavy rain.	
	5-8-17		Bn in billets in ST SYLVESTRE-CAPPEL. Preparations under Coy. arrangements.	
	6-8-17		Bn in billets in ST SYLVESTRE-CAPPEL. Parade under Coy. arrangements. O.P. Order received from Bde to march on following day.	
	7-8-17		Marched off at 8.0 A.M. and arrived at ROUGE CROIX at 9.45 A.M.	
	8-8-17		In Billets at ROUGE CROIX. Training under Coy. arrangements.	
	9-8-17		In Billets at ROUGE CROIX. Training under Coy. arrangements. Sports in afternoon. Draft of 6 O.R. joined for duty. Also 2 Lt B A J DUNLOP joined for duty.	
	10-8-17		Bn Paraded at 7.0 A.M. & marched to camp in No. 15 Area, BERTHEN, via METEREN.	

Army Form C. 2118.

WAR DIARY
or
INTELLIGENCE SUMMARY

(Erase heading not required.)

Instructions regarding War Diaries and Intelligence Summaries are contained in F. S. Regs., Part II. and the Staff Manual respectively. Title Pages will be prepared in manuscript.

Place	Date	Hour	Summary of Events and Information	Remarks and references to Appendices
In the Field	11-8-17		Bn in camp in BERTHEN. Parades under Coy arrangements. Draft of 7 Officers & 58 O.R. joined for duty.	
	12-8-17		Bn in camp in BERTHEN. Church Parades.	
	13-8-17		Bn in camp in BERTHEN. Range firing & parades under Coy arrangements	
	14-8-17		Bn in camp in BERTHEN. R.S.M.'s parade for Ceremonial in the morning. Commanding Officer's Ceremonial parade in afternoon.	
	15-8-17		Inspection of 90th Inf. Bde by Lieut Gen Sir HERBERT PLUMER, G.C.M.G., G.C.V.O., K.C.B., A.D.C.,	
	16-8-17		Bn in camp in BERTHEN. Warning order to move to KEMMEL SHELTERS on 20th inst. Gas demonstration & testing of Small Box Respirator in a gas cloud.	
	17-8-17		Bn in camp in BERTHEN. Parades under Coy arrangements. Draft of 1 Officer & 10 O.R. joined. Have to KEMMEL SHELTERS suspended	
	18-8-17		Bn in camp in BERTHEN. Church Parade. Parades under Coy arrangements. Draft of 9 O.R. joined for duty.	
	19-8-17		Bn in camp in BERTHEN. Church Parade.	
	20-8-17		Bn in camp in BERTHEN. Warning order to move on 22nd inst. Parades under Coy arrangements. Range firing.	
	21-8-17		Bn in camp in BERTHEN. Parades under Coy arrangements. Range firing.	
	22-8-17		Bn marched off at 7.30 A.M. passing the starting Point at 8.0 A.M. Route via WEST OUTRE & KEMMEL. Marched into camp just S. of the WYTSCHAETE-KEMMEL RD. about 1200 yds from KEMMEL at 11.30 A.M.	

Army Form C. 2118.

WAR DIARY
or
INTELLIGENCE SUMMARY
(Erase heading not required.)

Instructions regarding War Diaries and Intelligence Summaries are contained in F. S. Regs., Part II. and the Staff Manual respectively. Title Pages will be prepared in manuscript.

Place	Date	Hour	Summary of Events and Information	Remarks and references to Appendices
In the Field	23-8-17		Bn in camp near KEMMEL. Working Party of 150 in two small parties of 75 all ranks each found to work under 200th Field Coy. R.E. on DORSET STREET & BOB STREET C.T.s No Casualties.	
	24-8-17		Bn in camp near KEMMEL. Working Party of 300 in four small parties (A.B.C.&D) each of 75. all ranks found for work on C.T.s under 200th Field Coy. R.E. 1.O.R wounded. Draft of 6 O.R. joined for duty.	
	25-8-17		Bn in camp near KEMMEL. Same Working Party of 300 all ranks found. No casualties.	
	26-8-17		Bn in camp near KEMMEL. Church Parades. Same working party found. No casualties	
	27-8-17		Bn in camp near KEMMEL. Working Parties cancelled on account of Bad weather	
	28-8-17		Bn in camp near KEMMEL. Same working-parties. Warning order to move to BRISTOL CASTLE on 29-8-17. Draft of 7 O.R. joined for duty.	
	29-8-17		Bn marched off at 6.0 P.M. via SPY FARM & WULVERGHEM. Relieved 17TH Bn MANCHR Regt. Relief complete by 8.30 P.M. Whole Bn situated in trenches & shelters in vicinity of BRISTOL CASTLE.	
	30-8-17		Bn in vicinity of BRISTOL CASTLE. 3 working-parties found. 1). 1 Off. & 20 O.R. fuelling the trucks filled with R.E. material up Southern Tramway from WULVERGHEM DUMP to Bn HQ of 17TH Manch. Regt 2). 1 Off. & 50 O.R. fuelling trucks filled with R.E material up Northern Tramway from WULVERGHEM DUMP to BLAUWEN MOLEN DUMP. 3). 1 Off. & 50 O.R. working on dug-outs at 17 of Manch Regt H.Q. Draft of 1 Officer (2Lt J.A. ALLAN) & 5 O.R. joined for duty.	

Army Form C. 2118.

WAR DIARY
or
INTELLIGENCE SUMMARY.
(Erase heading not required.)

Instructions regarding War Diaries and Intelligence Summaries are contained in F. S. Regs., Part II. and the Staff Manual respectively. Title pages will be prepared in manuscript.

Place	Date	Hour	Summary of Events and Information	Remarks and references to Appendices
In the Field	31-9-17		Bⁿ in vicinity of BRISTOL CASTLE. Total of 280 all ranks found for work, in 5 small parties, one party carrying material to Front Line, one working on C.T.'s are constructing H.Q dug-outs for Right Bⁿ & are pushing trucks loaded with R.E. material from WULVERGHEM DUMP forward. Enemy Long-range guns active during night, firing on roads etc.	

H.F. ...field
Lieut. Colonel
[illegible stamp]

SECRET.

WAR DIARY.

for

SEPTEMBER 1917.

2nd. Bn. ROYAL SCOTS FUSILIERS.

[signature] Utterson Kelso Col¹
for Major.
Cmdg 2nd Bn. Royal Scots Fusiliers.

5.10.17.

Army Form C. 2118.

WAR DIARY
or
INTELLIGENCE SUMMARY.
(Erase heading not required.)

2nd BATTALION,
THE ROYAL SCOTS
FUSILIERS
O 3 6/1/4

Place	Date	Hour	Summary of Events and Information	Remarks and references to Appendices
In the Field	1-9-17		B[n] in vicinity of BRISTOL CASTLE. Some working-parties found as on previous night. Two parties were caught in shell-fire at 17th B[n] M.G.[r] H.Q. resulting in considerable casualties. Casualties:- 2nd L[t] N. DEWAR & 2L[t] A.C. WOOD wounded. 4 O.R. killed & 21 O.R. wounded. Warning orders to move on following day. Draft of 17 O.R. joined for duty.	
	2-9-17		B[n] marched off by platoons at 100 x interval, the first platoon moving at 7.0 A.M. The whole B[n] was clear by 8.0 A.M. B[n] marched via WULVERGHEM to a camp on the Southern slope of KEMMEL HILL. Vicinity of hill bombed by enemy during night.	
	3-9-17		B[n] in camp on KEMMEL HILL. Inspection parades. Vicinity of hill again bombed. A party of 3 Naval officers & 40 men visited the B[n] arriving about 5.0 P.M. They remained in the camp for the night. Officers names:- L[t] BRIDGE, L[t] BIRENQUET & Staff Surgeon LLOYD JONES.	
	4-9-17		The Naval Party was conducted to the WYTSCHAETE RIDGE in the morning, and shown the country in front and the old GERMAN lines. B[n] paraded at 6.30 P.M and marched off by platoons to a camp in the old support line about 1500 yds due West of WYTSCHAETE. B[n] settled by about 8.30 P.M.	
	5-9-17		B[n] in dug-outs & shelters in vicinity of CHINA WALL (W. of WYTSCHAETE). 2 day working parties & 1 night working party found, each party consisting of 2 officers & 100 men.	

WAR DIARY
or
INTELLIGENCE SUMMARY.
(Erase heading not required.)

Army Form C. 2118.

Place	Date	Hour	Summary of Events and Information	Remarks and references to Appendices
	6-9-17		working in the forward area on gun-pits & light railways.	
	7-9-17		Bn in vicinity of CHINA WALL. Same working-parties found.	
	8-9-17		Bn in vicinity of CHINA WALL. Same working-parties found.	
	9-9-17		Bn in vicinity of CHINA WALL. Same working-parties found. Draft of 15 O.R. joined for duty. Bn in vicinity of CHINA WALL. Church Parade. Same working-parties found. Orders received for relief of 2nd YORKS in support to 21st Bde in the line on night of 10th/11th & subsequent relief of 18th K.L.R. in the line on night of 11th/12th	
	10-9-17		Bn passed the Starting-Point near CHINA WALL in order D, C, B, A, H Q rs, the first platoon passing at 7.30 P.M. Bn took over from 2nd YORKS REGT (21st Bde) in support to 18th K.L.R. Left Bn in the line. A raid was expected & dispositions made accordingly but situation remained normal throughout the night. Vicinity of TORREKEN Fm was shelled at intervals. All Coys were situated between TORREKEN Fm & the WYTSCHAETE - MESSINES Rd	Map Ref. WYTSCHAETE Sheet 28 S.W.
	11-9-17		Bn moved out of support & relieved 18th K.L.R. in the line, commencing	

WAR DIARY
or
INTELLIGENCE SUMMARY.
(Erase heading not required.)

Army Form C. 2118.

Place	Date	Hour	Summary of Events and Information	Remarks and references to Appendices
	11-9-17		at 7.30 P.M. Relief reported complete at 12.10 A.M. 12TH Inst. Dispositions: 'D' Coy. Right Front Coy.; 'C' Coy. Left Front Coy.; 'A' Coy. Right Support Coy.; 'B' Coy. Left Support Coy.; Bn H.Q. at DERRY HOUSE. Frontage:- From JUNCTION BUILDINGS (O.17.c) where in touch with 69TH Bde on left, to BEEK FARM (O.29.b) where in touch with 18TH Manch'r Reg't on right. Method of Holding Line :- (1) The "Outpost line" consisting of a series of gunnel posts advanced to from 150 to 300x in front of (2). The "Piquet line", consisting of a nearly continuous line which however, requires a great deal of work. This is the main line of Resistance, & is reinforced from (3) The "Y LINE" a nearly continuous and fairly good line running between through squares 0.15. O.21 & O.27. The night was very quiet & the relief was carried out without difficulty.	Ref. WYTSCHAETE SHEET 28.S.W.

WAR DIARY
INTELLIGENCE SUMMARY

Army Form C. 2118.

Place	Date	Hour	Summary of Events and Information	Remarks and references to Appendices
In the Field	12-9-17		Day fairly quiet. Enemy did a certain amount of shooting behind PICQUET LINE with 5.9's & 4.2's. Observation was good, and our guns did a considerable amount of shooting.	
	13-9-17		Intermittent shooting was kept up all night by both sides. GUN FARM, roads & tracks and areas immediately behind front line were shelled by 5.9's, 4.2's & 77 mm shells. Day was fairly quiet. Observation was extraordinarily good. Casualties:- 1 O.R. killed, 2 O.R. wounded. Enemy aeroplane flew low over our left Coy. Picquet line just after "stand-down" in the morning and obtained fire for T.M.s Great air activity on both sides.	
	14-9-17		Same intermittent gun-fire during night. Hostile artillery very quiet during the day. Observation good. Great air activity on both sides again. About 2.0 P.M. an enemy squadron flew over at a great height. When over the WYTSCHAETE-MESSINES RIDGE, they turned & flew	

WAR DIARY or INTELLIGENCE SUMMARY

Army Form C. 2118.

Place	Date	Hour	Summary of Events and Information	Remarks and references to Appendices
In the Field	14-9-17		Back to their own lines, nothing known about every 200x between the edge & the BAY FARM ROAD about 3.30 P.M. one of our aeroplanes was shot down & crashed near POACHER'S POST. Observer seriously injured. Casualties:- 2 O.R. wounded.	
	15-9-17		A considerable amount of artillery fire on both sides during night, harassing roads & approaches to front line. Day fairly quiet. Casualties:- 2 O.R. Killed & 7 O.R. wounded.	
	16-9-17		Artillery active during night. Patrol located enemy post about 100x away from our No.9. Post. C.T. dug from Cox.H.Q.(WALL FM.) to PICQUET LINE. Our artillery carried out two practice barrages on our front, one at 10.0 A.M. and another at 4.0 P.M. Enemy retaliated, causing us a certain number of casualties. Casualties:- CAPT J.W.MERRY, wounded & duty. 9 O.R. Killed & 18 O.R. wounded	

Army Form C. 2118.

WAR DIARY
or
INTELLIGENCE SUMMARY.
(Erase heading not required.)

Place	Date	Hour	Summary of Events and Information	Remarks and references to Appendices
In Field	17-9-17		During night our Artillery carried out another practice barrage which drew very little retaliation. The usual night harassing fire was carried out.	
"	18-9-17		Day was quiet. Practice barrages were fired at night. Left of Div. Front. Again enemy retaliation was weak. Usual night harassing fire carried out by both sides. Our artillery carried out a practice barrage at 5.45 A.M. & 12.0 Noon. In both cases the enemy replied, but not very heavily, and only one casualty (wounded) resulted. Otherwise the day was quiet. Warning order received from Brigade to move to DENNY'S WOOD area of night of 21st/22nd into support of left Bde. Sector.	
"	19-9-17		Enemy artillery especially active around DERRY HOUSE and GUN FARM during night, the shells being chiefly used. Our artillery fired practice barrages at 6 a.m. & 3.0 P.M. Again enemy reply was very weak. Final Operation order for move to DENNYS WOOD.	

WAR DIARY
or
INTELLIGENCE SUMMARY.
(Erase heading not required.)

Army Form C. 2118.

Place	Date	Hour	Summary of Events and Information	Remarks and references to Appendices
In the Field	20-9-17		Night quiet. Very heavy Barrage opened by our guns at 5.40 A.M. The right of the Barrage fell about 300 x to the left of our left Coy. This turned out to be the Zero hour for a large attack North of us. Later on, word was received that the attack had been a great success and that all objectives had been captured with the exception of one or two gaps. The enemy did not retaliate on our front at all, and the whole day was extremely quiet. Casualties: 1 O.R. wounded & remained at duty.	
	21-9-17		Night quiet except between 3.0 & 4.0 A.M. when enemy shelled indiscriminately with gas shells & 4.2".	
	22-9-17		Batn. moved from Steenvoorde Road Line right Bks to Support Batn. left sector relieving 16th Manchester Regt. Bn. H.Q.'s at PENYL WOOD nr 164 of ESTAMINET CORNE and on the YPRES–COMINE line PARMA DUMP. Relieving two Coys is reserve of H.Q.'s	

WAR DIARY
or
INTELLIGENCE SUMMARY.
(Erase heading not required.)

Army Form C. 2118.

Place	Date	Hour	Summary of Events and Information	Remarks and references to Appendices
In field	23.9.17		Bn. found working parties nightly; 200 O.R. under R.E. for tramway, 35 O.R. for O.B.M. AVENUE under R.E., Cavalry Sentry, 10 O.R. to find Lewis Gun Posts. 5 O.R. Casualties. 2/Lt. J.A. SANGSTER, 2/Lt. G.A. LOW, 2/Lt. W.B. TAIT joined Bn. from Bn. Details. 27 O.R. Reinforcements.	
	24.9.17		Working parties as above. Intermittent shelling of Bn. H.Q. during night. No casualty.	
	25.9.17		Working parties as usual. 3 Casualties. Lt/Col Pillsbury during the day. Very hostile during night. 2/Lt. GANE slightly wounded in working party. 1 O.R. also wounded. Enemy in the Ypres Salient. 1 O.R. Casualty.	
	26.9.17		Working parties as usual. No Casualty.	
	27.9.17		Relieved & Cuffed by 16th MANCHESTER Regt. Bn. K.S.L.I. in the line. Bn. marched back to camp at N.25 b 67. (M.I. IRISH HOUSE).	
	28.9.17		Bn. found working parties 27. 150 O.R. nightly.	

WAR DIARY
or
INTELLIGENCE SUMMARY.

(Erase heading not required.)

Army Form C. 2118.

Place	Date	Hour	Summary of Events and Information	Remarks and references to Appendices
Fred	28.9.17		to work under R.E. O. Yard y Lines.	
	29.9.17		Training carried out by Bn during the day. Working parties as usual at night.	
	30.9.17		Halting parties for work in new helmet drill. Afterwards cricket & weights. 1 Platoon per Coy paid for a/c the 5th of the month. One working party during the night.	
	1.9.17		Night working parties to be continued. Lt. Cols. enough return during the night. Lt. Col. Campbell proceeded to England on leave. Coy officer returned from Brandhoek. Major J.C. Wyhan assumed command of Bn. Bn. 1/1 36 & B. Suf. 6 B. Middlesex	
	2.9.17		B.O.W. Coy. Bn. carried out training. New Coy en 1st and Bombing. Clothes and Lewis gun drill. Lewis guns were R.E. 3. Both 1st & 4 October available to carry on work.	

WAR DIARY
or
INTELLIGENCE SUMMARY.

Army Form C. 2118.

Place	Date	Hour	Summary of Events and Information	Remarks and references to Appendices
L Rueil	23.9.17		Evening arrived on duty Lieut. 2/Lt V.G. Walton and 4 O.R. reported from Fort MATILDA.	
	24.9.17		Heavy carried out during the day. C.O. parade in the afternoon.	

SECRET.

VOLUME 3. 35.A.

2nd R. SCOTS FUSILIERS
ORDERLY ROOM.
Date ....
No. Q.919/A

WAR DIARY

For

October 1917.

2ND. BN, ROYAL SCOTS FUSILIERS.

LIEUT. COLONEL,
COMDG. 2nd ROYAL SCOTS FUSILIERS.

WAR DIARY
or
INTELLIGENCE SUMMARY.
(Erase heading not required.)

Army Form C. 2118.

Place	Date	Hour	Summary of Events and Information	Remarks and references to Appendices
In the Field	5/10/17		Training carried out during the day. Officers' Reconnaissance to Ypres. Training work for night of 7th/8th	
" "	6/10/17		Raining interfered with training	
" "	7/10/17		Weather cold & rainy. C of E church parade. Presbyterian Church Parade cancelled on account of rain.	
	8/10/17		Practice attack cancelled on account of rain. Training carried out in camp	
	9/10/17		Practice attack carried out by "B". Ordinary Parades carried out by companies under their own arrangements	
	10/10/17		Companies parade under their own arrangements	
	11/10/17		The following officers joined the "B" for duty 2Lt J. MURRAY, 2Lt SHORT, 2Lt NELSON, 2Lt BAIRD, 2Lt BATTY-SMITH, 2Lt CAVEN. Capt. J. E. UTTERSON-KELSO M.C. takes over command of the "B". Major J. E. WILGHAM M.C. The "B" relieves the 18th B" King's LIVERPOOL REGIMENT in the line in the left B" sector	

WAR DIARY
or
INTELLIGENCE SUMMARY.

Army Form C. 2118.

Place	Date	Hour	Summary of Events and Information	Remarks and references to Appendices
In the field	12.10.17		B⁺⁰ in the line. D Coy — Right front Coy. C Coy — left front Coy. B Coy — Support. A Coy in Reserve. Headquarters at PRINZ RUPPRECHTS DUG-OUTS. Quiet day, misty. Two prisoners captured in front of D Coy. H pos. left front Coy. Casualties — 1 OR wounded. Major SHEPHERD 2nd i/c joins Bn 13⁺⁰ as 2nd in command.	
	13.10.17		Very quiet throughout the day.	
	14.10.17		Inter Coy relief carried out. A Coy to Right front, B to left front, C in support in OMEGA TRENCH, D Coy in reserve in OUSE trench. Casualties — 1 OR wounded.	
	15.10.17		Road & track areas shelled intermittently during the night.	

WAR DIARY
or
INTELLIGENCE SUMMARY.
(Erase heading not required.)

Army Form C. 2118.

Place	Date	Hour	Summary of Events and Information	Remarks and references to Appendices
	16/10/17		The Bn was relieved by the 16th Manchesters on the night of the 16/17th. Nr. Dispositions as follows. A Coy LUMM FARM B Coy, LANCASHIRE HOUSE. C Coy. CATACOMBS D Coy — RAILWAY DUMP. HD at TORREKEN FARM. Relief complete at 10.0 p.m.	
	17/10/17		DETAILS Coy under Lieut NISBET relieved the 18th Manchesters in the Right sub-sector on the night of the 17/18th Oct. Dispositions as follows, DETAILS Coy holding 4 posts in front line, with 4 posts in support. C Coy still at KILO FARM. C Coy went into reserve with Coy HD at HOW FARM. The remainder of the Bn (less D) in Support Bn area, as follows — A Coy at CATACOMBS B Coy at LANCASHIRE HOUSE, D Coy at RAILWAY DUMP. One Coy of 18th Manchesters at LUMM FARM. Bn Headquarters at TORREKEN FARM Bn HQ at BERRY HOPE	

WAR DIARY
or
INTELLIGENCE SUMMARY.
(Erase heading not required.)

Army Form C. 2118.

Instructions regarding War Diaries and Intelligence Summaries are contained in F. S. Regs., Part II. and the Staff Manual respectively. Title pages will be prepared in manuscript.

Place	Date	Hour	Summary of Events and Information	Remarks and references to Appendices
	18.10.17		Bn. in same position. Enemy artillery very active during the night. Our own the enemy.	
	19.10.17		The Bgde. The Bn. which were in support in DETAILS CAMP TORREKEN FARM and were relieved by the 2nd Bn. WILTS REGIMENT on the night of the 19/20th. The Coys. were to camp at VROILAND. Cord. R.M. Thornton left for England for duty with M.G. Corps. Major Shepherd (2nd in Command) assumes command. Capt. Achey Gryglow.	
	20.10.17		Enemy artillery very active on forward roads & tracks between 1 & 4 am. B. & D. Coys moved from VROILAND to HOEK CAMP. B. Coys near CHINA WALL — Stars Coy. C Coy. of Headquarters relieved from front support lines by 2nd WILTSHIRE REGT. & marched to CHINA WALL CAMP — N.23.a. Onest. night. Relief complete by 11.15 p.m.	
	21.10.17		Battalion reported present at CHINA WALL at 2 a.m.	

WAR DIARY
or
INTELLIGENCE SUMMARY.
(Erase heading not required.)

Army Form C. 2118.

Place	Date	Hour	Summary of Events and Information	Remarks and references to Appendices
	21.10.17		Late Reveille followed by cleaning up parades – German aeroplane over the camp early all the morning – no bombs dropped. C.O. holds conference with Coy. Offrs. – Church Parades for A, B & D Coys. C.O. attended conference of Bn & Bde HdQrs in the afternoon.	
	22.10.17		Close order training parades by Platoons – B Coy carries out special practice for proposed raid on a German Post. – Captn. J.K. Murray leaves Kegen as Assistant Adjutant. 2nd Lt. H. Nesbit assumes command of B Company. Lieuts. Moffatt & W.C. Mair parade acting rank of Captain whilst commanding companies. – Draft of 6 O.R. joins Battalion.	
	23.10.17	1 Off & 50 O.R. infantry rifle range re-camps. Co. wheels Camp arrives in turn. – Morrongo work much hindered by bad weather. – C.O. & Brigade Major inspect practice race ground 2nd Lt. J.T. Treacy rejoins from Base. – 2/27 Lt. Nesbit to Brig Card on Leave. – 2/16 D.R. Donnall assumes command of C Coy.	

WAR DIARY or INTELLIGENCE SUMMARY

Army Form C. 2118.

Place	Date	Hour	Summary of Events and Information	Remarks and references to Appendices
	24.10.17		1 Offr & 50 OR hutting near camp – 1 Offr & 25 OR building range near Brigade HQrs – Brigades rents camp Tres road practice by B Coy – 2nd in Command & Coy Cdrs of A C & D recce STAMP POST CORNER recommended boundary end of Survivors Reserve Line (between HON FM & JESPAGUE CM) found engineers & french digging to be done there the night 25/26 & Oct. C.O. Owed up plans with B Coy for raid on enemy front Capt J R Murray assumes duties of A/Adjutant	
	25.10.17		A C & D Coys carry out practice for Survivors digging task – B Coy for raid A C & D Coys proceed to boundary end of line between HON FM & DESPAG N° FM & extend 60 yds of trench to the South. Good moonlight – trench completed by 10 P.M. Coys back in camp by midnight	
	26.10.17		Heavy wet day – Coys held special training – Lectures in tents	

Army Form C. 2118.

WAR DIARY
or
INTELLIGENCE SUMMARY.
(Erase heading not required.)

Place	Date	Hour	Summary of Events and Information	Remarks and references to Appendices
	27.10.17		Presentation of Ribands by General Sir AYLMER HUNTER – WESTON, Commanding VIII Corps, Sir J. Rumbold – as follows:	
			CAPTAIN (now MAJOR) J.E. UTTERSON KELSO M.C. – Bar to M.C	
			2.Lt. (A/Capt.) J. GILCHRIST. Military Cross.	
			40781 Cpl. (A/Sgt.) J. TELFORD D.C.M	
			22513 Pte C. Graham "	
			19467 Pte. C. Sutherland Military Medal	
			20326 Pte W. Paton "	
			7369 Pte R. Bell "	
			11867 Pte J. Tiernan "	
			8567 Pte J. Best "	
			18359 Pte Macdermett "	
			40543 Cpl J. Bell "	
			7732 Sgt W. Waldiewicus "	
	28.10.17		Bn. moved into support at TORREKEN FARM relieving 2nd Bn YORKSHIRE REGT.	

WAR DIARY
or
INTELLIGENCE SUMMARY.
(Erase heading not required.)

Army Form C. 2118.

Place	Date	Hour	Summary of Events and Information	Remarks and references to Appendices
			Bn. H.Qrs. Bty. at CUMA Fm. B. Coy at LANCASHIRE HOUSE	
			C Coy at CATACOMBS. D Coy swung to flanked Kensington Railway	
			Jump thrown at CHINA WALL	
	29.10.17		Relieved 2nd Bn WILTSHIRE REGT in left sector. Dispositions —	
			Bn Hqrs Right Coy. B Coy Left Front Coy. C Coy in Support at	
			OMEGA TR. D Coy in Reserve at OUSE TRENCH	
	30.10.17		Quiet night - with clear moonlight. Pot at 0170 bombarded	
			by 20 German Minnies & by bombs. Scattered shelling on	
			back areas during afternoon.	
	31.10.17		2 Officers & 2 men of B Coy wounded by a raid from No 11 Pot.	
			On enemy dug outs. At 6.30am run how. they found the enemy	
			already prepared with 3 M.G's & had burnt down a Support	
			line Gravelin - One O.R killed Same my O, one enemy attempt	
			on the pot was made chewing off with casualties. 2 O.R.	
			wounded in OMEGA TRENCH	

SECRET.

WAR DIARY.

for

NOVEMBER 1917.

2ND BN. ROYAL SCOTS FUSILIERS.

5.12.17.

[signature] Lieut-Colonel.
Commdg 2nd Bn Royal Scots Fusiliers.

Volume X

S E C R E T.

W A R   D I A R Y.

for

N O V E M B E R   1917.

2ND BN. ROYAL SCOTS FUSILIERS.

[signature]
Lieut-Colonel.

5.12.17.   Commdg 2nd Bn Royal Scots Fusiliers.

Army Form C. 2118.

WAR DIARY
or
INTELLIGENCE SUMMARY.
(Erase heading not required.)

Place	Date	Hour	Summary of Events and Information	Remarks and references to Appendices
	1.11.17		Battalion relieved in Left Sub Sector by 16th Bn Manchester Regiment. Scenery relief practised at O.17 central and reached by those square of enemy in single file. The garrison, morning reconnoissance drove off the attack by Lewis Gun, Rifle & Bomb. B" moved into Brigade Support at TORREKEN FARM AREA. Disposition — A Coy LON M FARM. B Coy — LOW CASHIRE HOUSE. C Coy CATACOMBS. D Coy — RAILWAY DUMP & in dugouts on road near CATACOMBS. 1 Platoon was detailed for keeping manured reserve.	
	2.11.17		Battalion supplied a Guard of Honour for General Plumer at BAILLEUL.	
	3.11.17		Fairly Quiet day. 1 Aeroplane fowler down 11.30 am & fired M.G. at RAILWAY DUMP and LANCASHIRE HOUSE. Transport shelled on way up from LAMP POST CORNER to RAILWAY DUMP 1 limber delayed. TORREKEN FARM shelled from 9 am – 11 am with H.V guns B" gas into Regt Liaison, relieving 16th B" Manchester Regt Dispositions — C Coy Front Line. C Coy — Right Support at MANCHO HOUSE. A Coy Left Support at HEN FARM. 1 Platoon B Coy in Reserve at CABIN HILL.	Lieut-Colonel R.S.S. Commanding 2nd B.

Army Form C. 2118.

WAR DIARY
or
INTELLIGENCE SUMMARY.
(Erase heading not required.)

Instructions regarding War Diaries and Intelligence Summaries are contained in F. S. Regs., Part II. and the Staff Manual respectively. Title pages will be prepared in manuscript.

Place	Date	Hour	Summary of Events and Information	Remarks and references to Appendices
	1.11.17		Bn in Bivouac followed on by Bn had taken by to be Marching Regiment. Enemy relief put at Div wind now wears uniform of revival of anger. The Germans making transport easy. The schools 14 Bavn, Gren. Regt & Gren., 55 moved into Bulgaria, Supply at Torres q farm area. Continuing — Bty comm. narrow. 13 cpl Weasling house coy coverbs Bty — R-1-ny Dump Bcoy in cup B Tea 5 hrs 13 cup catsioloists theatre are inside n using to in two not in uniform. Evans to the new for fresh against caminé. 20 milieu.	
	2.11.17		Fairly Quiet day. E. Aeroplane launches when Landmarks had Mg on Railway Dump was Longcoatche House soaring at shelled on way up from 40 m. Post Coffers in army / D.m.c. B. the discharged.	
	3.11.17		Turkey farm sullen from firm at Humble post 2y 30 — gun over Right Infantry Infantry 16" on Maxell ay 2 & farm in C coy. Trophies C coy Right Support at Moncho House a coy in supports at hm Farm 1 Platoon Bcoy in Reserve at Chord Hill. Rarg Callie 130	

WAR DIARY
or
INTELLIGENCE SUMMARY.
(Erase heading not required.)

Army Form C. 2118.

Place	Date	Hour	Summary of Events and Information	Remarks and references to Appendices
	5.11.17		Quiet day & night. A few gas shells at DERRY HOUSE about 9pm. Patrol of 1 Offr & 12 O.R. got in touch with enemy working party, 50 strong, & after m.g. fire, had to withdraw.	
	6.11.17		Heavy barrage on left. Patrol out from No 2 Post heard large enemy working party. Our artillery active during day.	
	7.11.17		Patrol going out, fired on working party near Rifle Farm, waited for 10 minutes and again fired. They then withdrew under m.g. fire. Enemy heavies active behind DERRY HOUSE about 3 am. 6 bombs fell in vicinity of Bn H.Qrs. & MESSINES ROAD. Bn relieved in Right Subsector by 2nd Bn WILTSHIRE REGT. Relief completed by 9.35 pm. Bn moved to VROIL ANDHOEK CAMP.	
	8.11.17		Enemy aeroplanes active in area about 3 am. Bombs dropped in Transport Lines. Casualties: 1 O.R. killed. 2 wounded. Gas shelling. Cleaning up. Warning order received for Bn to move to STRAZEELE on 11th November.	

WAR DIARY
or
INTELLIGENCE SUMMARY.
(Erase heading not required.)

Army Form C. 2118.

Instructions regarding War Diaries and Intelligence Summaries are contained in F. S. Regs., Part II. and the Staff Manual respectively. Title pages will be prepared in manuscript.

Place	Date	Hour	Summary of Events and Information	Remarks and references to Appendices
	9.11.17		Attached American Officer leaves B" accepted medically by M.O. Training Parade.	
	10.11.17		Inspection of B" by Commanding Officer.	
	11.11.17		Bn marches from VROILAND HOEK CAMP to billets at ROUGE-CROIX, near STRAZEELE. Marched off at 9 a.m. — in billets by 3.30 p.m.	
	12.11.17		Training took place in troops. Clean up of Foot, Superior, R.S.M's Parade in the afternoon.	
	13.11.17		Drill from 9-12 by Coys. R.S.M's parade in afternoon. Rugby match with 16th Manchester Regiment. Result 3 points each.	
	14.11.17		B" moves by bus from ROUGE-CROIX to STEENVOORDE Area.	
	15.11.17		Coy training in forenoon 2-3 p.m. R.S.M's parade	
	16.11.17		Coy training Games from 7 a.m. — 7.45 a.m. & 9 — 12.30. Afternoon devoted to Musketry. Sunn Officers leave to join Heavy M.G. section.	
	17.11.17		Coy Parades training 7.0-7.45 a.m. 9-12.30 p.m. R.S.M's parade 11.30 — 12.30. "Blue Birds" read B" at night.	
	18.11.17		Church Parade "Blue Birds" at night. Cleaning up of dress requirements.	

Army Form C. 2118.

WAR DIARY
or
INTELLIGENCE SUMMARY.
(Erase heading not required.)

Instructions regarding War Diaries and Intelligence Summaries are contained in F. S. Regs., Part II. and the Staff Manual respectively. Title pages will be prepared in manuscript.

Place	Date	Hour	Summary of Events and Information	Remarks and references to Appendices
	19.11.17		Coy training & Recreation.	
	20.11.17		As above.	
	21.11.17		Route march by A.C., B Coy. B & D Coys company training.	
	22.11.17		Route march for B & D Coys. Warning order received for B" to proceed to RENINGHELST & thence to MENIN ROAD "Blue Bands" at night.	
	23.11.17		Coy training. Divisional General inspects Battalion.	
	24.11.17		B" moves by march route to ONTARIO CAMP, near RENINGHELST. Reconnoitring party visits the line.	
	25.11.17		B" moves by light railway from FUZEVILLE SIDING, RENINGHELST to MANOR HALT, near ZILLEBEEK, & there relieve 4th/5th Royal Highlanders at BODMIN COPSE. Dispositions — B" HQrs., A, B & D Coys at BODMIN COPSE. C Coy under orders of 16th B" manned a Regt. 1dles left of left Subsector. Immediately S. of SCHERRIABEEK 3 Offrs & 100 O.R. form armament working party & lived at RAILWAY DUGOUTS. Machine guns & [active] forward tracks. 1 O.R. killed; 3 wounded.	

WAR DIARY or INTELLIGENCE SUMMARY

Army Form C. 2118.

Place	Date	Hour	Summary of Events and Information	Remarks and references to Appendices
	26.11.17		Quiet day. 3 men wounded on working parties.	
	27.11.17		A Coy relieves C Coy in line. 1 O.R. killed, 1 wounded.	
	28.11.17		BRITISH BODMIN COPSE heavily shelled from 5–6 a.m. probably retaliation for our previous barrage. 5 O.R. wounded.	
	29.11.17		Enemy Artillery & Machine Guns active on back areas during concentration on POLDERHOEK CHATEAU. A Coy not being relieved we were able to bring effective Rifle + L.G. fire on a large party forming up moving from broken stuff, inflicting heavy casualties. A no. of casualties observed. 1 O.R. died of wounds. B Coy relieves A in line.	
	30.11.17		13th Hepn + Support Coys again heavily shelled. Attempted strong raid on B Coys right flank at dawn was repelled, known enemy casualties – 6 killed 4 wounded.	

WAR DIARY

Of The

2ND BATTALION ROYAL SCOTS FUSILIERS.

FOR THE MONTH OF DECEMBER 1917.

31.12.17.

L.T. Shepherd
Major.
Commanding 2nd B Royal Scots Fusiliers.

Army Form C. 2118.

WAR DIARY
or
INTELLIGENCE SUMMARY.
(Erase heading not required.)

Instructions regarding War Diaries and Intelligence Summaries are contained in F. S. Regs., Part II. and the Staff Manual respectively. Title pages will be prepared in manuscript.

Place	Date	Hour	Summary of Events and Information	Remarks and references to Appendices
In the Field	1.12.17		Continued practice shoot by our artillery. A Coy relieved by D Coy - 2 O.R. wounded. Enemy working party caught by Lewis gun fire - 2 killed, 4 wounded.	
" "	2.12.17		Quiet day. Officers of 19th Regt. Wexford Regt. visit to reconnoitre.	
" "	3.12.17		New Zealand Brigade attack POLDERHOEK CHATEAU at 12 noon. Our Company in left attack withdrawn and take up position again at night. Bn relieved by 19th K.L.R. machine gun Coy - 5 O.R. killed, 2 died of wounds, 23 wounded. to MANOR HALT and entrain for ONTARIO CAMP. Casualties 3 killed, 6 wounded. Total Casualties	
	4.12.17		Rest cleaning up.	
	5.12.17		Training under Coys.	
	6.12.17		Coy Training carried on on schemes drawn up by Coy Cdrs.	
	7.12.17		As before. Any improvements carried out under supervision of officers detailed	
	8.12.17		As before. Warning order to proceed to trenches.	
	9.12.17		Church Parade. Cleaning up.	
	10.12.17		Training under Coy Arrangements. Camp improvements carried on. D/Lieut M Urquhart Leave for machine gun Corps. Intelligence Officers reconnoitre Bn's line position at TORR TOP. Entraining arrangements made.	

WAR DIARY or INTELLIGENCE SUMMARY

Army Form C. 2118.

Place	Date	Hour	Summary of Events and Information	Remarks and references to Appendices
Lastre Field	12.12.17		Bn entrained at FUZEVILLE siding proceeding by rail to MANOR HALT and by march route to TORR TOP where it relieved the 17th Bn Kings Liverpool Regt. Casualties Nil. Working Party of 2 Offr & 100 OR carrying materials up to front line - Casualties of party 1 OR Killed 1 OR wounded.	
"	13.12.17		Carrying party of 1 Offr & 35 OR working on obtaining of pill-boxes. Remainder of Battn in TORR TOP tunnels. Bombs constantly bursting in area of attack reconnoitred 85 OR on working parties during the night. 2/Lt A. Campbell speared from Signalling Course. Draft of 43 OR joined for duty.	
"	14.12.17		O.C. A Coy proceed from TORR TOP to reconnoitre route to left Battn outpost, preparatory to our relieving 18th B Manchester Regt. On arriving at Bn HQ (18th Manchester) they learned that the things had occurred and were holding about 300 yards of the front line WEST of POLDERHOEK CHATEAU. C.O. called to attend a Consultation at Brigade H.Q. at STIRLING CASTLE. At 1.45 pm orders received from BD that A Coy should proceed at once to reinforce and support 18th Manchesters who were to counter-attack in the evening. A Coy moved off and O.C. Coy reported to O.C. D Coy of Manchesters in the immediate support trench. More carried out successfully in daylight and Casualties. At 3 pm further orders received from C.O. that remainder of Battn the Alpha Shenll move up in fighting order to proceed	

Army Form C. 2118.

WAR DIARY
or
INTELLIGENCE SUMMARY.
(Erase heading not required.)

Place	Date	Hour	Summary of Events and Information	Remarks and references to Appendices
In the Field	14-12-17		Position. Coys. moved off in order C. D. B. coys. with following dispositions:- C Coy formed A Coy. D Coy in shell holes in rear of forward Bn. HQ. B Coy in reserve at CLAPHAM JUNCTION and MENIN ROAD. Rations dumped at TORR TOP and carried to forward coys by D Coy. Between 7.30 p.m. & 8 p.m. a bombing attack by the 18th Manchesters supported by A & B coys was carried out resulting in clearing the Huns out of Captured trench. 17 K.L.R. moved into reserve at TORR TOP. Casualties:- mgt 1 O.R. killed, 1 O.R. wounded. Lieut E. Johnston & 2/Lt A. Gilson joined Bn. for duty. Deft of 4 O.R. joined for duty.	
" "	15.12.17		D Coy moved back into TORR TOP at 5 a.m. and occupied tunnel vacated by one Coy of 17 K.L.R. Huns counter-attacked and owing to exhaustion of supply of bombs we were unable to maintain our position and were forced to retire to our original starting-point. Our Casualties were:- Killed. 2 offrs 24 O.R., Wd & Missd. 1 officer & 101 O.R., Wounded 5 O.R. Missing 3 O.R. 18th Manchesters relieved by us and two Coys. of 17th Manchesters under Capt Woodward. Dispositions:- A Coy. which was A Coy cloth up position on left, C Coy on left centre, B Coy right centre with 17th Manchester on right. Large parties of bombs, SAA carriers brought up to trenches. E Each leading up to front line was heavily	

WAR DIARY or INTELLIGENCE SUMMARY

Army Form C. 2118.

Place	Date	Hour	Summary of Events and Information	Remarks and references to Appendices
In the Field	15-12-17		Shelled throughout the night and casualties occurred amongst carrying parties of the 17th King's Regt. Situation in front line very quiet. Draft of 2 O.R. joined for duty.	
"	16.12.17		Situation remained quiet all day. Bn in 2 coys of 17th Manchesters relieved by 2nd Bn M/Ch's. Relief complete about 10 pm. Bn H.Q. & B. Coy moved to HEDGE STREET trench. A Coy to CANADA ST TUNNEL, B Coy to MOUNT SORROW, D Coy to ILLIAD TRENCH. Waived to move to ONTARIO CAMP on following day. Casualties on this date 1 O.R. missing, 4 O.R. wounded. 2nd Lieut D.M. Nelson wounded remained on duty. Total Casualties on tour Killed 3 O.R., 6 O.R. A.J. H. & D.O.W. 13 O.R. missing, 40 O.R. wounded.	
"	17.12.17		Weather very cold & frosty. Bn relieved by 10th Kings Liverpool Regt. Marched to MANOR HALT and entrained for ONTARIO CAMP arriving at FUZEVILLE SIDING about 7 pm.	
"	18.12.17		Day spent in rest, cleaning up and making good deficiencies. Weather cold & frosty.	
"	19.12.17		Bn inspected by C.O. Major Stephens set out by lorry to obtain foodstuffs for mens Xmas dinner. 2nd Lt J.L. Riddell leaves for Musketry Course at HAYLING ISLAND.	
"	20.12.17		A Coy & B coys attended baths at WESTOUTRE. All Lewis Gun teams fired on range. Camp visited at 12.30 pm by an American General who inspected men at dinner. Major Stephens returns with large load of foodstuffs.	
"	21.12.17		Weather still very cold, misty & frosty. All bombers carried out bombing practice and	

WAR DIARY or INTELLIGENCE SUMMARY

Army Form C. 2118.

Place	Date	Hour	Summary of Events and Information	Remarks and references to Appendices
In the Field	21.12.17		Organisation under 6 Stn Reorg on ground at Brigade School at M+ C.H.Q. from 10am-1pm. Training of Lewis Gunners in camp. Wiring carried out by riflemen, class other than specialists.	
"			Lieut A. Fitzsimon reports for duty.	
	22.12.17		Bombing practice & organisation carried out by Corp. Fox. Rifles at range carried out by Lewis Gunners. Remainder of Coys. Coys out wiring & coy training.	
"	23.12.17		Bn moves to TORR TOP TUNNELS by tram from FUSEVILLE SIDING to MANOR HALT thence by march route relieving the 19th Kings Liverpool Regt. Relief complete about 4 pm. Working parties found on arrival.	
	24.12.17		Bn relieves 2nd Bedford Regt in the left Battn sub-sector. Relief complete about 8pm without any casualties. 18th Manchester take over from us in TORR TOP. Hostile artillery very active on E. Track.	
			Lying up to front line from Bn H.Q. Area around TOWER HAMLETS heavily shelled at intervals throughout the night.	
	25.12.17		Hostile artillery very active at intervals throughout the day. Hostile M.G. fire very active on tracks. Enemy aircraft flew very low over our lines apparently taking photographs, although very heavily engaged by L.G. A.A. fire.	
	26.12.17		Hostile artillery active in morning but quieter than usual at night in a few active on tracks.	

WAR DIARY
or
INTELLIGENCE SUMMARY.
(Erase heading not required.)

Army Form C. 2118.

Place	Date	Hour	Summary of Events and Information	Remarks and references to Appendices
Sh Jule	26.12.17		Casualties inflicted on enemy by our Lewis Gunners & rifles during 2 suspected relief. Both areas shelled by gas shells at night. Disposition of Bn when in front line. A Coy + 1 Platoon of B and 1 Platoon C in support. 2 Platoons C in support. 2 Platoons of B in right Support Strong points. C in left support Strong points. 2 Platoons of B in right Support Strong point. Casualties 2 O.R. wounded.	
"	27.12.17		Hostile Artillery normal throughout the day. Bn relieved by 16th Manchesters. Rgt. Relief complete at 9pm. Heavy M.G. fire encountered along E Road and at STIRLING CASTLE. a heavy bombardment of gas shells was encountered. Various working parties found by Battn on arrival at STIRLING CASTLE.	
"	28.12.17		Bn visited by 2/i/c Command and Officers of the 12th Rifle Brigade belonging to 20 Division. STIRLING CASTLE area reconnoitred by them preparatory to their incoming early in January. Practically nil (with working parties in forward area. 1 O.R. wounded.) Casualties during Bn in 3. O.R. wounded.	
	29.12.17		Bn relieved in STIRLING CASTLE by 19th K.R.R. Relief complete at 5 pm. Bn entrained at MINOR HALT for ONTARIO CAMP	
	30.12.17		Cleaning up & making good deficiencies of kit. Bathing parades at CHIPPEWA CAMP Sergt Major HQ the Capt Officers regular Commission into late C.vi pools to C.O. E.H. Smith reported for duty was posted to A Coy.	
	31.12.17		Bathing parades for other HQrs. Feet Inspection of B, D, D Coys by M.O. Eye Examn of Bn inspections through cleaning up of arms, equipment etc. a busy training.	

L. S. Shepherd
LIEUT.-COLONEL,
COMDG. 2nd ROYAL SCOTS FUS.

Volume 3.

WAR DIARY
OF
THE 2ND. BN. ROYAL SCOTS FUSILIERS.
FOR PERIOD.
JANUARY 1 - 31st 1918.

4.2.18.

Lieut-Colonel.
Commanding 2nd Bn. Royal Scots Fusiliers.

Army Form C. 2118.

WAR DIARY
or
INTELLIGENCE SUMMARY.
(Erase heading not required.)

Place	Date	Hour	Summary of Events and Information	Remarks and references to Appendices
In the Field	1-1-18		Picketing and clearing up. All the men of the battn. and horses to dinner at 1 pm in the YMCA hut RENINGHELST and attended at regimental concert immediately after dinner.	
" "	2-1-18		General cleaning up of equipment, rifles etc preparatory to our move on 3rd Jany.	
" "	3-1-18		Coys C.A. Dis inspected by Major Shepherd at following hours - A Coy 10 a.m., B. Coy 10.20 a.m., C Coy 10.40 a.m. A Coy 11 a.m. Others at 11.30 a.m. Orders received from Brigade re leaving and attaining orders to Butts, visited by General Douglas Smith, also Tuesday, now commanding the 2nd Division & have accompanied by General Williams C.O.C. 30th Division.	
" "	4-1-18		Training under Coy arrangements.	
" "	5-1-18		Bn marches from ONTARIO CAMP to DICKEBUSCH SIDING entraining there at 11 a.m. Detraining at EBBLINGHAM at 4 pm whence it marched to billets in BLARINGHEM area. Billets very scattered. Warned of inspection from 9th Corps to XVII Corps.	
" "	6-1-18		Rest & cleaning up prior to move on following day.	
" "	7-1-18		Bn marches to STEENBECQUE STATION entraining at 3 pm. Arrived at LONGUEAU STATION Kindly after 11 pm. While men were filling tea, a Coy under Capt McKenzie detailed to carry out the unloading of Divisional trains for next five days. Capt Lof Mercy, MGC in turn in charge of detaining of better for marches from LONGUEAU at 12.15 a.m. to FULLOY, a distance of 6 Kilometres, arriving in billets at 7 a.m.	

Army Form C. 2118.

WAR DIARY
or
INTELLIGENCE SUMMARY.
(Erase heading not required.)

Instructions regarding War Diaries and Intelligence Summaries are contained in F. S. Regs., Part II. and the Staff Manual respectively. Title pages will be prepared in manuscript.

Place	Date	Hour	Summary of Events and Information	Remarks and references to Appendices
In the field	8-1-18		Battn. resting after previous days travelling	
"	9-1-18		Parade under Coy arrangements. Much discipline fire, foot drilling and march order of marching 3 abreast	
"	10-1-18		Parade under Coy arrangements. R.S.M. parade at 2 p.m.	
"	11-1-18		Parade by companies. Warning Order received to move to ROSIERES	
"			Nesle area.	
"	12-1-18		Usual parades under Coy arrangements. Route to ROSIERES reconnoitred	
"	13-1-18		Bn marches from Fouilloy at 7 a.m. at head of Brigade column & arrives at ROSIERES at 1 p.m. Distance of march approx 12 miles. Test inspection on arrival	
"	14-1-18		Bn parade at 9 a.m. & marches to Languevoisin 2½ kilometres E. of Nesle. Arrived at 2.35 p.m. having a distance of 9 mile (appx) halt 4 & 2 hr after had just returned from there. Test inspection on arrival	
"	15-1-18		Parades from 10 a.m to 12 noon from 2 - 3 p.m. Parades included cleaning up, handling of arms, march discipline & test inspection. Brigade arrange for route signalling to take place next day between chalk sheets at NESLE & about 500 y N. of V. in LANGUEVOISIN.	

WAR DIARY
or
INTELLIGENCE SUMMARY.
(Erase heading not required.)

Army Form C. 2118.

Place	Date	Hour	Summary of Events and Information	Remarks and references to Appendices
O. the field	16-1-18		Training carried out by Battalion as laid down in letter No G.679.	
	17-1-18		R.S.M's parade from 2pm - 3pm. Lt. E. Hotewell (?) with overseers Command of "C" Coy. Parades carried on as laid down in letter No 9,678 for 3 days Programme. A Coy trained Lewis Gunners fired on Range from 10am - 12 noon. B Coy from 2pm - 4pm.	
	18-1-18		Training carried on as laid down for 4th days programme in letter G.678. R.S.M's parade from 2pm - 3pm. B Coys trained Lewis Gunners fired on Range from 2-3pm. A Coy Bombardiers conference to discuss new form of training as laid down by 2nd & VIIIth Corps.	
	19-1-18		Training carried on as laid down by the Commanding Officer at previous days conference. Baths were allotted to Coys as follows to A Coy 9am - 10am. D Coy 10am to 12 noon & B Coy from 2pm - 5pm.	
	20-1-18		Baths allowed to A Coy from 9am to 12 noon & B Coy from 2pm - 5pm. Divine service for Bn. at 11 am.	
	21-1-18		Baths for B Coy from 9am - moon having carried out as per programme arranged by Coy Commanders.	

WAR DIARY or INTELLIGENCE SUMMARY

Army Form C. 2118.

Place	Date	Hour	Summary of Events and Information	Remarks and references to Appendices
In the Field	23-1-18		Coy/Squadrons carry out their own programme.	
" "	24-1-18		Training by Coys. C.O. proceeds by Car at 6 am to reconnoitre the line to be taken over by us from the French Orders received for move to Granater.	
" "	25-1-18		Training by Coys under the supervision by O.C. Coys.	
" "	26-1-18		Regt. marches from LANGUEVOISIN at 5.45 am to GRANDRU - arriving about 12.30 pm, a distance of about 25 kilometres. Feet inspection & rest to following days move.	
" "	27-1-18		Regt. marches from GRANDRU to PERSEMAND, and lost halting place before going into the line. O.C. Coys & Intelligence officer go straight into line to reconnoitre & take over from the French.	
" "	28-1-18		Regt. relieves the 22nd Dragons 5th French Cavalry Division in the right Sub-Sector (Barisis) Relief complete at 9 pm Dispositions in the line are:- "A" Coy, with one platoon "C" Coy, in close support on right front line HO at FAISE. "B" Coy, with one platoon of "C" Coy, in Support of "B" Coy in LE CLOS on left front with HO at STATION. One platoon of	

WAR DIARY
or
INTELLIGENCE SUMMARY.

(Erase heading not required.)

Army Form C. 2118.

Place	Date	Hour	Summary of Events and Information	Remarks and references to Appendices
In the field	28.1.18		DE VIGNES. Move with Bn HQ at LES REDOUTS. "A" Coy in Reserve at LES KARRIERES BERNAFOURG. Situation quiet. No casualties during relief	
"	29.1.18		Situation generally quiet. Front line shelled slightly in the afternoon in reply to our artillery fire on right of Bn. Raid carried out by the Bosch on our right at 5pm, 3 prisoners being secured.	
	30.1.18		Situation very quiet	
	31.1.18		Situation still quiet. Weather misty, note observation difficult. Capt DB McKenzie M/C Gen: proc: leave Base on a 6 months tour of duty in U.K.	

[signature]

LIEUT. COLONEL,
COMDG. 2nd ROYAL SCOTS FUSILIERS

WAR DIARY

of the

2ND BATTALION ROYAL SCOTS FUSILIERS.

FOR THE MONTH OF FEBRUARY 1918.

4-3-18.   Lieut-Colonel.
         Commanding 2nd Bn. Royal Scots Fusiliers.

WAR DIARY
or
INTELLIGENCE SUMMARY.
(Erase heading not required.)

Army Form C. 2118.

Place	Date	Hour	Summary of Events and Information	Remarks and references to Appendices
In the Field	1-2-18		Batts still in the line in BARISIS sector. Enemy artillery slightly more active. Cannot manning fronts in any sector.	
" " "	2-2-18		Situation still quiet. British artillery complete relief with French. The Second in command & 2 Coy commanders of 8th Bn LONDON Regt, 174 Bde, 58th Dn. visit the Bn. in order to see the sector, preparatory to taking over. Inter-company reliefs take place, "C" Coy relieving "A" Coy on the right front, "D" Coy relieving "B" Coy on left front. "B" Coy moving back to Reserve in BERNAGOUSE, "A" Coy to the Redoubt. Reliefs carried out without any casualties.	
" " "	3-2-18		Enemy artillery much more active than on preceding days. One 2 the French battery positions in rear bombarded with gas shells.	
" " "	4-2-18		Situation generally quiet. Work carried out on strong points in rear. One patrol active defense moved the Cemetery in front of supporting sector, finding it unoccupied and no trace of the enemy seen. Quite French working parties Bde for duty.	

WAR DIARY
or
INTELLIGENCE SUMMARY.
(Erase heading not required.)

Army Form C. 2118.

Instructions regarding War Diaries and Intelligence Summaries are contained in F. S. Regs., Part II. and the Staff Manual respectively. Title pages will be prepared in manuscript.

Place	Date	Hour	Summary of Events and Information	Remarks and references to Appendices
In the field	5.7.18		Enemy artillery activity below normal. Nout at night still carried on throughout Bn sector. Two patrols went out during the night, but no signs of the enemy. Lieuts & Leard, 2/Lo Fraser and Templeton return from Brux EO.	
" "	6.7.18		Situation very quiet. 2/Lt O.L. Riadd reports from abroicite in England. 2/Lo Fraser & Templeton take over command of D & B Coys respectively. Casualties 1 O.R. DoW, 7 O.R. wad (accidental).	
" "	7.7.18		Situation quiet. Operation orders received for relief of Bn by 8th London on night of 9th/10th.	
" "	8.7.18		Situation still quiet. Various points in sector shelled slightly throughout the day. 2/Lt. Baird, Warren & Short leave for course of Instruction.	
" "	9.7.18		Bn relieved by 9th Bn London R.Gt, marched back by Coys to Merville ago of Marielle Bichancourt billeting.	
" "	10.7.18.		Bn march to Puchoir's freezy starting from - at 9.30 a.m., arriving - at 7 p.m.	
" "	11.7.18.		March continued from Puchoir to Liberinent in Enchew area, reaching	

Army Form C. 2118.

WAR DIARY
or
INTELLIGENCE SUMMARY.
(Erase heading not required.)

Instructions regarding War Diaries and Intelligence Summaries are contained in F.S. Regs., Part II, and the Staff Manual respectively. Title pages will be prepared in manuscript.

Place	Date	Hour	Summary of Events and Information	Remarks and references to Appendices
In the field	11-2-18		cont. There about 1 p.m. Reconstitution of 90th Inf Bde Troops, viens Coyats of 2nd Bedfords, 2nd R.S.F. & 16th Manchester Regt.	
" "	12-2-18		Ceremonial Parade of Division in preparation for visit of G.O.C. 2nd C.	
" "	13-2-18		30th Division inspected by Sir Douglas Haig, in the vicinity of Behen, morning spent in cleaning equipment etc. The G.O.C. arrived at 3.45 pm, & after inspection, the 21st Sq. & 90th Inf Bdes marched past the saluting base. The G.O. expressed his pleasure at the smartness of the troops.	
" "	14-2-18		Training carried out under platoon commanders. The G.O. O.C. Coys & Intelligence proceed to Rouppy, to make a reconnaissance of sub sector. Leave in Cousand Two Coy Officers proceed by bus to reconnoitre route:–	
			MON-EN-CHAUSSEE	
" "	15-2-18		G.O. conference with Coy & Platoon Commanders regarding training. Field manoeuvres by XVIII Corps.	
" "	16-2-18		Training carried on under Coy Commanders. Chiefs tactical exercises on under 5.O. Intelligence Officer, 2 + 6 Sn's proceed by bus to ESTREILLERS, thence by foot to reconnoitre "G" Sub-sector of Batt. Zone.	

Army Form C. 2118.

WAR DIARY or INTELLIGENCE SUMMARY.

Army Form C. 2118.

(Erase heading not required.)

Instructions regarding War Diaries and Intelligence Summaries are contained in F. S. Regs., Part II. and the Staff Manual respectively. Title pages will be prepared in manuscript.

Place	Date	Hour	Summary of Events and Information	Remarks and references to Appendices
In the Field	17-2-18		Church service at 11.30 am. Capt. & Qm. Spence goes to hospital. 60 pieces	
" "			to Ham to attend a five-days conference at Corps HQ re Extraordinary	
" "			accounts temp. command of Battn.	
" "	18-2-18		Training carried out by Coys. Capt. W.J. Newton takes over the duties	
" "			of Adjt. vice Capt. R. Newey on leave. Warning order received for Battn.	
" "			to proceed to forward area.	
" "	19-2-18		9 am - 12 noon tactical schemes carried out by Coys under arrangements	
" "			of Coys. 2 pm - 3 pm R.S.M's. parade.	
" "	20-2-18		By bus 9 officers & 400 OR who go ahead in lorries to form a working	
" "			party at Aubigny, marches from Liéramont via Ham to Villers St	
" "			Christophe. to O's regime Battn.	
" "	21-2-18		Whole Bn. are working parties in the vicinity of Aubigny. Working	
" "			parties received for move to any dug-outs the following day, preceded	
" "			D. coys. sub-sector.	
" "	22-2-18		Bn. marches from Villers St Christophe to Savy dug-outs, leaving at 9.25	
" "			am, + arriving at 1 pm.	

WAR DIARY or INTELLIGENCE SUMMARY

Army Form C. 2118.

(Erase heading not required.)

Place	Date	Hour	Summary of Events and Information	Remarks and references to Appendices
On Feb	23-2-18		Battn engaged in digging trenches in D. North Sub Sector of Battle Zone	
"	24-2-18		Work continued as on previous days. Mostly function coppices cut by 08 Coy	
"	25-2-18		Continuance of digging trench schemes carried out in Battle Zone. A + B Coys starting manning their positions. C + D Coys forming the attacking force.	
"	26-2-18		Note on Sub-sectr contained: Northern order for which A + B Coys holding Res in forward Zone. Kept Peterborough + White Horse Barrier rating rooms & kept Reps respectively. C + D still engaged in digging trenches. C.O. + 2nd in Command the forward position often taking over. Relief took place to any casualties. Enemy Inactive. Sent is in Battle station later place.	
"	27-2-18		Relief of 3rd Ben Hants Regt by Batln. Leaving Foresham + Henley brewery was C.30 p.m. Followed by Westlecove station. Relief completed 10.30 p.m. Without any casualties. Maj W.S. Shephen Regne Bn from Hospital	

W. Wilson K.b
LIEUT. COLONEL,
2nd ROYAL SCOTS FUSILIERS.

90th Inf.Bde.
30th Div.

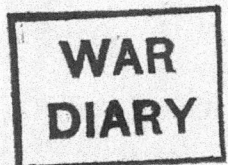

2nd BATTN. THE ROYAL SCOTS FUSILIERS.

M A R C H

1 9 1 8

30/-

2 R. Scots Fus
Feb
Vol XV

from VII w Dec
vice 19. Mich

16.A.
8 books

VOLUME 3.

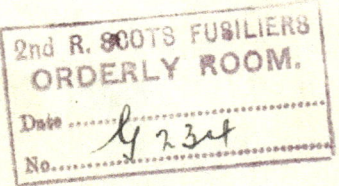

WAR DIARY

OF THE

2ND BATTALION ROYAL SCOTS FUSILIERS.

FOR THE MONTH OF MARCH 1918.

             Lieut-Colonel.
3-4-18.   Commanding 2nd Bn Royal Scots Fusiliers.

WAR DIARY
or
INTELLIGENCE SUMMARY.
(Erase heading not required.)

Army Form C. 2118.

Place	Date	Hour	Summary of Events and Information	Remarks and references to Appendices
In the field	1-3-18		Day spent in preparing for move from Sans Dugouts to Forward Zone. Leaving Coy learnt Sans at 6.30 pm. Disposition as follows "B" Coy on right front, "D" Coy on left front, "A" Coy (centre) 2 Platoon in Francilly & 2 Platoons close to St Quentin Railway, "C" Coy (Reserve Coy) beside Batt HQ in BROWN QUARRY. Relief completed by 10.30 pm. No casualties.	
" "	2-3-18.		Situation quiet. Two of the enemy approached one of our posts during the forenoon, but were fired on, and retreated to to hit. This was dropped his gas mask, which was recovered, rendered identification obvious.	
" "	3-3-18		Enemy attitude generally quiet. Observation rendered difficult owing to the inclemency of the weather. Left front sector slightly shelled from 4.30 am during an attempted enemy raid on the Batt on our front. Left. About 9 pm a strong part of the enemy attempted to raid the centre post of D Coy on OLD ROMAN ROAD, but were unsuccessful. He suffered a casualties. Enemy losses unknown.	

Army Form C. 2118.

WAR DIARY
or
INTELLIGENCE SUMMARY.
(Erase heading not required.)

Instructions regarding War Diaries and Intelligence Summaries are contained in F. S. Regs., Part II. and the Staff Manual respectively. Title pages will be prepared in manuscript.

Place	Date	Hour	Summary of Events and Information	Remarks and references to Appendices
In field	4-3-18		Situation general quiet	
"	5-3-18		Improvement in weather. Our artillery carried out harassing fire on enemy fronts in enemy's line. Patrols proceeded to TERRIERS to reconnoitre defences.	
"	6-3-18		Bn relieved by 2nd Bn YORKSHIRE REGT. Relief complete by 10.40 pm. Battn proceed to ETREILLERS	
"	7-3-18		17th Bn MANCHESTER REGT relieves Battn in ETREILLERS after which the Bn marched via FLUQUIERES, & AUBIGNY to DURY, leaving at 5.40pm & arriving at 9pm. Capt FETHERSTONHAUGH & 2 other Officers attend a demonstration of tank projectors at FLUQUIERES. 60 prisoners commencing officers schemes during the afternoon	
"	8-3-18		Day spent in cleaning up Equipment, clothing etc.	
"	9-3-18		Training carried out according to 1st Divn Programme. 60 attend a scheme during the day	
"	10-3-18		Church service in field & opening Orderly Room at 11 am	

WAR DIARY or INTELLIGENCE SUMMARY.

Army Form C. 2118.

Place	Date	Hour	Summary of Events and Information	Remarks and references to Appendices
	11.3.18		Training carried on under Coy. supervision. C.O. attends practice counter-attack scheme.	
	12.3.18		Coy. training continued.	
	13.3.18		Gymkhana held by Battalion outside DURY	
	14.3.18		Coy. training continued. C.O. again attends scheme with Coy. officers. Genl. Sir Douglas Smith visits "B".	
	15.3.18		Coy. training.	
	16.3.18		Coy. training continued.	
	17.3.18		Voluntary Church Services	
	18.3.18		"B" marches to ETRELLERS via AUBIGNY - FORESTE. Relieves 2nd YORKS. Regt. in defended locality. Practice manning of battle positions.	
	19.3.18		Practice manning of Battle Positions early in the morning. Quiet day.	
	20.3.18		Own artillery somewhat active, especially at night. 2nd. Lt. Knight Bruey wounded.	
	21.3.18		Intense enemy barrage opens at 4.40 a.m. Battle positions manned. Strong attack develops at 10.0 a.m. MANCHESTER REDOUBT still holding out at 4.30 p.m. fell presumably about 6.30 p.m. as no further news from 16th Manchrs.	
	22.3.18		Attack on Battle Zone held by 2nd BEDFORDS. "A" Coy. R.S.F. moved up to replace	

WAR DIARY
or
INTELLIGENCE SUMMARY.
(Erase heading not required.)

Army Form C. 2118.

Place	Date	Hour	Summary of Events and Information	Remarks and references to Appendices

counter attack Coy. of BEDFORDS reorganised in the fighting. A Coy of 18th K.R.R. replaces "A" Coy. "A" Coy. makes a successful counter attack at 1 p.m. in trenches N. of SAVY-ETREILLERS Road. 2nd LT J. MURRAY wounded. At 2 p.m. enemy again retake trench. New fourth attack under 2nd LT J. BLAIR temporarily successful, but Coy. is too weak to hold on. 2nd LT J. BLAIR wounded. Remains of Coy. withdraw to ETREILLERS. CAPT. W.C. NAIR, O.C. "B" Coy, killed by a sniper. Enemy drawing down on both flanks. Orders received at 4.30 p.m. to withdraw & proceed to 14 A.M. Withdrawal began in good order at 4.40 p.m. with enemy snipers & M.G. gunners making their way thro ETREILLERS. "B" makes its way in small parties thro. H.A.Q to VERLAINS much orders to bivouac there. LT HAKEWELL-SMITH & No 5. Platoon of 'B' Coy did not get orders to withdraw, & remained in forward position, holding off enemy until dark. They then marched on a compass bearing, thro VAUX & GERMAINE already held by the enemy, & though challenged twice by parties of the enemy, made their way successfully to H.Q. Arrived there at 5 a.m.

WAR DIARY or INTELLIGENCE SUMMARY

Army Form C. 2118.

Place	Date	Hour	Summary of Events and Information	Remarks and references to Appendices
	23.3.18		At 4.30 am heavy M.G. rifle fire near HAM caused B" while stood to. At 6 am it was checked broke up in a different direction.	
			VERLAINE – ESMERY-HALLON Road, 2nd Bedfords on right, ourselves on left. Quiet day, except for a good deal shelling on positions. Orders received to move up to fill up flank towards DOLANCOURT. Move postponed.	
	24.3.18		B" ordered forward at 4.45 am. Patrols immediately in contact with enemy 2nd Lt H.S. Bryce wounded. Our immediate flank was pursued at 7 am & withdrawal ordered to ESMERY-HALLON defences. Delaying action fought along the road, heavy casualties being inflicted on the enemy working in force round our left flank. Coys retreated from B" HdQrs in direction of VILLETTE – new position near FLAVY-le-MELDEUX, where they reorganised & fought a delaying action, & finally under orders withdrew to ROIEGLISE which they reached at 12 noon 25th. Rearguard fired by B" HdQrs. late last night. Meanwhile, about 11 am withdrawal was made by B"Coys along with 2nd Bedfords to ESMERY-HALLON defences already under fire from our field guns, reached by them	

Army Form C. 2118.

WAR DIARY
or
INTELLIGENCE SUMMARY.
(Erase heading not required.)

Place	Date	Hour	Summary of Events and Information	Remarks and references to Appendices
	24.3.18 (continued)		with orders that the village, intending to make for the Canal defences at LIBERMONT. On the way thro' the village, CAPT. R.H. THOMAS, R.A.M.C. was killed. Immediately west of ECOFAY HALLON, elements of 90th Bde were formed with other mixed units into three or four skirmishing lines, & these gave mutual protection until the bridge at LANNOY FARM was safely crossed. The next line was immediately organised into posts of mixed units under senior officer as were available, the 90th Bde sector being E. of LANNOY FARM Sector S. of the bridge was relieved by elements of French troops during the night.	
	25.3.18		About 11 a.m. the battle developed along the whole front, but a strong resistance was made, though the Pretrow was heavily enfiladed by M.G. & field guns fire. About 2:30 p.m. the French on our right retired, & the left flank being turned, others were received from Bde to with draw. This was done, but was very difficult owing to the marsh marsh behind & the heavy enfilade fire. Two rallies were attempted, but nothing could be done, & the survivors of the Division were driven by SOLENTE	

WAR DIARY
or
INTELLIGENCE SUMMARY.
(Erase heading not required.)

Army Form C. 2118.

Place	Date	Hour	Summary of Events and Information	Remarks and references to Appendices
	25.3.18	(cont'd)	to ROIEGLISE, where O.C. Hd.qrs. & Coys. reunited & were reorganised. "B" bivouaced here. Bn. conveyed by bus to ARVILLERS.	
	26.3.18		At 11 a.m. Bn. was ordered to advance along the ROYE-AMIENS Road & take up a defensive position at LE QUESNOY. Enemy was in possession, & it was decided to make a stand at BOUCHOIR, with 89th Bde on left & BEDFORDS, R.S.F. astride the road, & 36th DIV. on the right. All afternoon, cavalry patrols were visible in front of the Batalion. Towards nightfull, transport, infantry & artillery were seen moving our front in the direction of ERCHES, about 3000x from our outposts. At 11 p.m. a section of transport missed their way, came into our lines. The personnel killed or taken prisoner, & 1 field kitchen, 1 water cart & two G.S. wagons captured.	
	27.3.18		About 10 a.m. a strong attack developed both right & left, and by 12 noon both flanks being turned, we had to withdraw to about 800x west of ARVILLERS - LA FOLIE road. A counter attack was immediately organised, and under heavy M.G. fire advance was made to a position 40x west of the road, and our outposts on it &	

Army Form C. 2118.

WAR DIARY
or
INTELLIGENCE SUMMARY.
(Erase heading not required.)

Place	Date	Hour	Summary of Events and Information	Remarks and references to Appendices
	27.3.18	(cont'd)	in front of trenches B Coy O.I.R. During the advance Lt MACKENZIE SMITH 2/Lt McMILLAN Lt K MACKENZIE, 2nd Lts J. SANGSTER and P MARION were wounded. Coy right fell back & was organised with 18th Kings L.R. on left, R.S.F. centre, 9 BEDFORDS right. During the night the trench were taken over no	
	28.3.18		By 6.0 am only 30 trench had arrived in the position, which they afterwards remained as an outpost line, but drove decided to hang on. Strong attacks developed on Lt FOLIE (left) & ARTILLERS. Fight by 10.0 am our front was opened from 11.0 am many casualties being caused by a field gun being brought almost at 800x level was removed from the 89th Bde on left that they were to consider themselves relieved without dream on one, Our right flank was turned, but extensive flank was formed, & a sharp rifle fire was brought to bear on the enemy until about 2 pm S.A.A. ammunition was practically exhausted & word was now received that we were relieved & were without but to minimise casualties, it was decided to hang on till dusk. Immediately afterwards however, it was found that the BEDFORDS	

Army Form C. 2118.

WAR DIARY
or
INTELLIGENCE SUMMARY.
(Erase heading not required.)

Instructions regarding War Diaries and Intelligence Summaries are contained in F.S. Regs., Part II. and the Staff Manual respectively. Title pages will be prepared in manuscript.

Place	Date	Hour	Summary of Events and Information	Remarks and references to Appendices
	26.3.18.	(cont'd)	9 R.S.F. were alone in the trenches, with the enemy far round on the right; the order to withdraw was given. During this, we suffered numerous casualties from M.G. & field gun fire. 2 2nd Lts. A.R. DOUGAL & N. TEMPLETON were missing. The Bn marched to ROVREL, & remained there in close billets all next day.	
	29.3.18.		At ROVREL, in reserve to 4th French Cavalry Division. Ordered to take up CANTONNEMENTS des ALERTES at MAILLY. Order cancelled.	
	30.3.18.		At 8.30 am ordered to march to SALEUX, where Brown entrained for ST VALERY S. SOMME.	
	31.3.18.		Arrived at S. VALERY at 1.0 am & marched 5 kilos to ARREST.	

Milley Rees
LIEUT. COLONEL,
9TH BATTN. ROYAL SCOTS FUSILIERS.

WO95/2340
2/14 London
(London Scottish)
June '18 – Aug '19